100 Instagram Strategies to Grow Your Real Estate Business

Dedication

To my husband, Mallesh Budugu — Your unwavering support, love, and belief in me have been the foundation of this journey.

You stood by me through every challenge, inspired every bold move, and reminded me of my strength when I doubted it most. Your faith gave me wings to dream big and the courage to turn those dreams into reality.

This book is not just a reflection of strategy and growth— It is a tribute to the power of partnership, love, and the quiet strength that lifts us higher.

Thank you for being my greatest cheerleader and my strongest pillar.

— Maheshwaree Budugu

Preface

These 100 strategies are drawn from real-world experiences and marketing principles that work. My goal is simple: help you grow your real estate brand through one of the most powerful platforms of our time.

Welcome to *Instagram Digital Marketing Strategies for Real Estate* — your comprehensive guide to mastering Instagram as a powerful tool for growing your real estate business. In today's fast-paced digital world, traditional marketing alone no longer guarantees success. Instagram, with its vast global user base and engaging visual format, offers unparalleled opportunities to connect with potential buyers, sellers, and investors.

This book is designed to help real estate professionals, whether you are a seasoned agent or just starting out, leverage Instagram's features—from posts and Stories to Reels, Ads, and Analytics—to build brand awareness, generate leads, and close deals. Throughout these 100 pages, you will find practical strategies, actionable tips, and real-world examples tailored specifically for the real estate market.

My goal is to empower you with the knowledge and tools needed to navigate Instagram's dynamic landscape confidently and creatively. Let this book be your companion as you embark on a journey to elevate your marketing, engage your audience, and ultimately grow your real estate business.

With love and dedication,

— Maheshwaree Budugu

Introduction

In recent years, Instagram has transformed from a simple photo-sharing app into a robust platform that shapes how businesses engage with customers. For the real estate industry, Instagram offers unique advantages: the ability to showcase stunning property visuals, tell compelling stories, and build a loyal community—all within a mobile-friendly, highly visual environment.

However, succeeding on Instagram requires more than just posting attractive images. It demands a well-planned strategy, consistency, and an understanding of how to use Instagram's tools to their full potential. This book addresses these needs by breaking down the essential elements of Instagram marketing for real estate—from optimizing your profile and creating engaging content to using ads and analysing results.

Whether your goal is to increase brand visibility, attract qualified leads, or enhance client relationships, this book will guide you step-by-step in crafting an effective Instagram marketing plan. Each page is crafted to be concise yet insightful, making it easy for you to implement strategies immediately and measure their impact.

This book is designed as a blueprint—step-by-step strategies you can use regardless of your current following. Whether you're trying to boost engagement, generate leads, or convert followers into clients, you'll find targeted methods here.

Remember, consistency beats perfection. Implement these strategies at your own pace, track your growth, and optimize what works best for your audience. Remember, consistency beats perfection. Implement these strategies at your own pace, track your growth, and optimize what works best for your audience.

Let's begin your Instagram success journey.

CONTENTS

SECTION 3: Growth Tactics (Pages 61–100)

SECTION 4: Monetization (Pages 100–127)

SECTION 5: Advanced Strategies (Pages 128–167)

SECTION 6: Success Stories & Final Thoughts (Pages 168–187)

Page 1: Why Instagram is a Game-Changer for Businesses

In today's fast-paced digital world, Instagram has become more than just a photo-sharing app—it's a powerful marketing engine driving real business results. With over **2 billion active users worldwide**, Instagram gives businesses an incredible platform to connect directly with their target audience, showcase products or services, and build a strong brand presence.

One of the biggest reasons Instagram is a game-changer is its **visual-first nature**. People process visuals 60,000 times faster than text, making it easier for businesses to grab attention with compelling images, videos, reels, and stories. For industries like **real estate, fashion, fitness, or food**, where visuals matter the most, Instagram becomes the perfect digital showroom.

Another major benefit is **engagement**. Instagram consistently has one of the highest engagement rates among all social platforms. Users actively like, comment, save, and share content, giving businesses the chance to create relationships—not just reach. It's not just about followers anymore; it's about building a community.

Instagram also offers **free and paid marketing tools**—from detailed analytics to shopping features, clickable story links (for accounts over 10k), and targeted ad campaigns. These tools allow you to track performance, optimize strategies, and generate qualified leads or direct sales right from the app.

The rise of **Reels and short-form video** has further transformed how brands tell stories. Even small businesses can go viral with one creative video, levelling the playing field and enabling rapid organic growth without a huge ad budget.

In short, Instagram helps businesses become **discoverable, desirable, and trusted**. Whether you're a solopreneur or a big brand, leveraging Instagram smartly can fuel brand growth, lead generation, and sales like never before. If you're not yet using Instagram to grow your business, you're missing out on a golden opportunity in the digital age.

Page 2: Creating a Winning Business Profile

Your Instagram profile is your digital storefront—it's the first impression users get of your brand. In less than five seconds, visitors decide whether to follow you, engage with your content, or move on. That's why creating a winning business profile is critical for success.

Start with your **profile picture**. Use a high-quality logo if you're a brand or a clear, professional headshot if you're a personal brand. Make sure it's recognizable and consistent across all platforms for better brand recall.

Next, craft a compelling **bio**. You have only 150 characters, so make it count. Clearly state who you are, what you offer, and who it's for. For example: *"Helping first-time home buyers find their dream property | DM for free consultation."* Emojis can make it visually engaging, but don't overdo it.

Your **username and handle** should be easy to remember, searchable, and brand-aligned. Avoid using too many dots, underscores, or complex words. If your business name is taken, try adding a relevant keyword like your city or service.

Don't ignore the **website link**. This is your only clickable link, so use it wisely. You can direct it to your website, landing page, WhatsApp, or a link aggregator like Linktree or Beacons to showcase multiple destinations.

Set your profile to a **Business or Creator account** to unlock access to analytics, promotional tools, and CTA buttons like "Contact" or "Book Now." This boosts professionalism and functionality.

Finally, organize your **story highlights**. Treat them like a mini-website: "About Us," "Reviews," "Listings," "FAQs," etc. Use custom cover icons to maintain a clean aesthetic.

In essence, your Instagram profile should be clear, trustworthy, and inviting. A well-optimized profile builds instant credibility and encourages profile visitors to become followers—and eventually, customers.

Page 3: Bio Optimization for Maximum Conversions

Your Instagram bio may seem like a small detail, but it plays a massive role in converting profile visitors into loyal followers and potential clients. Think of it as your digital elevator pitch—short, sharp, and convincing.

To optimize your bio, start by clearly identifying **what you do** and **who you help**. Avoid vague or generic statements. Be specific. For example, instead of saying "Helping people grow," say "Helping real estate agents get 30+ qualified leads/month through Instagram."

Include a **value proposition**. This is your "why"—what's in it for the visitor if they follow or contact you. For example: "Free home buying checklist inside!" or "DM 'START' to book your free strategy call."

Break your bio into **clear, scannable lines**. Use line breaks, emojis, and bullet points to enhance readability. A typical structure could look like this:

🏠 Real Estate Growth Expert
📱 Helping Realtors Scale with Instagram
🎯 DM "LEADS" for Free Strategy Call
👇 Grab Your Free Toolkit

Make smart use of your **call-to-action (CTA)**. Your CTA should guide users on what to do next—visit your website, download a freebie, join a webinar, or DM a keyword. This increases engagement and drives conversions.

Utilize the **Name Field** for keywords. It's searchable and can boost discoverability. Instead of just using your name, try something like "Ankit | Real Estate Marketing."

Finally, keep your bio updated with any time-sensitive offers or events, like "🏆 Masterclass this Sunday | Book Now!"

Remember: Your Instagram bio isn't just a description—it's a sales tool. Treat it like a billboard that invites the right people into your world. A well-optimized bio can turn casual visitors into warm leads, and warm leads into paying clients.

Page 4: Choosing the Right Username & Handle

Your Instagram username (also known as your handle) is one of the first elements people see, and it plays a key role in searchability and brand identity. Choosing the right username isn't just about looking good—it's about making your business easy to find, remember, and trust.

Start by choosing a handle that reflects your **brand name** as closely as possible. If you already have a business name or domain, try to match that on Instagram. For example, if your company is called "Elite Property Hub," your handle should ideally be @elitepropertyhub.

If your exact name is unavailable, don't worry. Add **relevant keywords** like your service or location:

- @elitepropertyhub.mumbai

- @eliteproperty_expert

- @eliteproperty.india

Avoid using excessive punctuation, numbers, or random symbols. A username like @john_doe_9823__realty may be available, but it's not professional or easy to remember. Simplicity is key.

Make sure your **username is consistent** across platforms. This improves brand recognition and builds trust. If someone searches your business on Instagram after seeing your website or Facebook, they should find the same name.

Use the **Name field (not the handle)** to improve search discoverability. For example, in the name field, write: "Ankit | Real Estate Advisor" instead of just "Ankit." Instagram's search feature uses the name field more than the handle, so take advantage of this space for keywords.

Once you pick a handle, stick to it. Frequent changes confuse your audience and harm your brand's consistency. Secure your username early—even if you're not ready to fully use Instagram yet.

Remember: Your handle is your brand's digital identity. A clean, keyword-friendly, and memorable username can enhance trust, searchability, and overall professionalism—making it easier for your ideal audience to find and follow you.

Page 5: How to Create a High-Converting Link in Bio

Instagram allows only one clickable link in your bio—this makes it **prime real estate** for lead generation and conversions. Used strategically, this single link can become a traffic machine that drives users to your sales funnel, lead magnet, or booking page.

Instead of sending users to a generic homepage, direct them to a **specific, goal-oriented destination**. Ask yourself: what action do I want users to take after visiting my profile? Book a call? Download a free guide? View listings? Your link should align with that objective.

A high-converting strategy is to use **link-in-bio tools** such as:

 Linktree

 Beacons

 Stan Store

 Solo.to

These tools let you showcase multiple clickable links within a mobile-optimized page. For example, you can include links like:

- 🏠 View Property Listings

- 🎯 Book Free Consultation

- 🧲 Download Lead Magnet

- 📞 Contact on WhatsApp

To increase conversions:

1. Use **clear CTA buttons** like "Tap to Book a Call" or "Get Free Checklist."

2. Add your **brand logo** and profile picture for trust.

3. Keep the layout **simple and mobile-friendly**—most traffic will come from mobile users.

If you prefer more control, create a **custom landing page** on your website instead of using third-party tools. This can improve branding and allow you to capture email leads directly.

Don't forget to **track your link clicks** using tools like Bitly or built-in analytics on platforms like Beacons and Linktree. Knowing what users click on helps you refine your strategy.

Ultimately, your bio link is your silent salesperson. Done right, it guides visitors down your conversion path, turning curiosity into action—and action into sales.

Page 6: Understanding Instagram's Algorithm

To grow and succeed on Instagram, it's crucial to understand how the **Instagram algorithm** works. It's not your enemy—it's a system designed to show users content they're most likely to engage with. When you align your strategy with the algorithm, your content gets seen by more people, boosting visibility, engagement, and conversions.

The algorithm is not one single formula. It behaves differently based on content type: feed posts, stories, reels, and explore page each have **unique ranking signals**. However, the core principle across all areas is **engagement**—likes, comments, shares, saves, DMs, and time spent on your content all matter.

Here's how the algorithm prioritizes content:

◆ **Relevance:** The algorithm shows users content that aligns with their past behaviour and interests.

◆ **Relationship:** Accounts you interact with often—through likes, comments, or DMs—are favoured.

◆ **Timeliness:** Newer posts are shown higher in the feed. Posting when your audience is active helps.

◆ **Engagement Rate:** The more interactions your post gets in a short time, the more it's boosted.

◆ **Content Type:** Videos, especially Reels, tend to get more reach if they align with trending formats.

Reels are currently Instagram's top priority. They're pushed more aggressively, especially if they use **trending audio**, hook viewers in the first 3 seconds, and retain attention for most of the video.

To "beat" the algorithm:

✓ Post consistently (at least 3–5 times per week)

✓ Encourage interactions (ask questions in captions, use polls in stories)

✓ Use relevant hashtags and location tags

✓ Create content that saves and shares easily

✓ Analyze insights and refine what works

Understanding and cooperating with the algorithm isn't about chasing trends—it's about creating value-packed, authentic content that sparks interaction.

Page 7: Business vs Creator Account – What to Choose

One of the first decisions you'll need to make when setting up your Instagram for marketing is whether to choose a **Business Account** or a **Creator Account**. Both are part of Instagram's professional suite and come with powerful features, but the right choice depends on your brand type, content goals, and monetization strategy.

◆ **Business Account: Best for Brands and Companies**

This is ideal for service providers, real estate firms, product-based businesses, agencies, and storefronts. Key features include:

- **Contact buttons** (Call, Email, Directions)
- **Instagram Shopping** integration
- Access to **Meta Ads Manager** for advanced ad targeting
- **Insights** on audience behavior and post performance
- Ability to connect with **third-party scheduling tools** (like Buffer, Later, or Hootsuite)

A Business Account is perfect if you want to run paid ads, collect leads, and scale a company or product through professional tools.

◆ **Creator Account: Best for Influencers and Personal Brands**

This option is designed for content creators, influencers, coaches, and freelancers. It provides:

- More **detailed follower growth insights**

- Flexible **category labels** like "Public Figure," "Motivational Speaker," etc.

- **DM filter tools** for better organization

- Access to branded content tools (for influencer partnerships)

If your brand is tied closely to your **personality or face**, a Creator Account offers more nuanced tools for community building and content tracking.

❗ Important Note:

Both accounts give you access to Reels, analytics, Instagram Insights, and allow you to use music for content creation. The **key difference** lies in ad options, shopping features, and backend organization.

Page 8: Setting Goals for Instagram Growth

Setting clear, actionable goals is the foundation of any successful Instagram strategy. Without goals, your efforts can become scattered and ineffective. When you know what you want to achieve, every post, story, and interaction becomes purposeful, driving your real estate business closer to growth and profitability.

Start by defining **what success looks like** for your Instagram presence. Common goals include:

- Increasing brand awareness in your target market

- Generating qualified leads for property sales or rentals

- Building a loyal community of engaged followers

- Driving traffic to your website or landing pages

- Booking consultations or property viewings through Instagram

- Growing your email list for long-term nurturing

- Your goals should be **SMART**—Specific, Measurable, Achievable, Relevant, and Time-bound. For example:

- "Gain 1,000 new followers in 3 months with 5% engagement rate"

- "Generate 20 qualified leads per month via Instagram DMs"

- "Increase website visits from Instagram by 30% within 6 weeks"

Once you set your goals, break them down into smaller milestones and tasks. For example, to get more leads, you might:

- Post 3 Reels per week targeting first-time buyers

- Host a weekly Instagram Live Q&A about buying property

- Use targeted hashtags related to your local market

- Run a paid ad campaign to promote free consultations

Tracking progress is critical. Use Instagram Insights to monitor metrics like follower growth, reach, engagement, website clicks, and DM inquiries. Adjust your strategy based on what's working and what isn't.

Page 9: Identifying Your Target Audience

Understanding your target audience is the cornerstone of effective Instagram marketing. When you know exactly who you want to reach, you can tailor your content, messaging, and advertising to resonate deeply, which leads to higher engagement and better conversions.

Start by creating a detailed **audience persona**. This is a fictional profile representing your ideal customer. For a real estate business, consider factors like:

- **Demographics:** Age, gender, location, income level, education

- **Psychographics:** Interests, values, lifestyle, motivations

- **Needs & Pain Points:** What challenges do they face in buying or selling property?

- **Behavior:** What type of content do they consume? When are they online?

For example, your target audience could be: "Professionals aged 28-40 in Mumbai looking for their first apartment, interested in home décor, finance, and family lifestyle content."

Use Instagram's **Insights** tool to analyze your current followers. Look for trends in who engages most with your posts and stories. This data helps refine your persona and content strategy.

Next, research your competitors and industry leaders. Who are they targeting? What hashtags do they use? What content resonates with their audience? This competitive analysis gives clues on how to differentiate yourself.

Tailor your content specifically to address your audience's needs. If you're targeting first-time home buyers, create posts explaining the buying process, budgeting tips, and neighborhood reviews. If you focus on luxury properties, highlight exclusivity, design, and lifestyle.

Engaging with your target audience is equally important. Respond to comments, DMs, and questions promptly. Use polls and quizzes in stories to learn more about their preferences.

In summary, knowing your target audience allows you to create meaningful, relevant content that builds trust and encourages action—making your Instagram efforts more efficient and effective.

Page 10: Content Pillars for Real Estate Instagram

Creating consistent, valuable content is easier when you organize your posts around core **content pillars**—the main themes that define your brand and attract your target audience. For real estate businesses, well-planned content pillars help build authority, engage followers, and drive conversions.

Here are five effective content pillars for a real estate Instagram account:

1. **Property Listings and Showcases**
   Highlight new and featured properties with professional photos, videos, and virtual tours. Use carousel posts or reels to show multiple rooms and amenities. Add compelling descriptions focusing on benefits and unique features.

2. **Educational Content**
   Share tips and advice related to buying, selling, financing, and investing in real estate. This could include mortgage explanations, market trends, legal tips, or home maintenance guides. Educational content positions you as a trusted expert.

3. **Client Testimonials and Success Stories**
   Social proof builds credibility. Post photos, videos, or quotes from satisfied clients, along with brief stories about their journey and how you helped. This humanizes your brand and encourages trust.

4. **Behind-the-Scenes and Personal Branding**
   Show the people behind the business. Share day-in-the-life posts, team introductions, office culture, or your personal story. This creates connection and relatability, making followers feel more connected to you.

5. **Community and Lifestyle**
   Feature local events, neighborhoods, restaurants, schools, and lifestyle spots near your listings. Highlight what makes the community special. This content appeals to buyers imagining their future lifestyle.

Balancing these pillars keeps your feed engaging and informative. Use a mix of images, videos, reels, stories, and live sessions to diversify content formats and boost reach.

Having clear content pillars streamlines your content planning and ensures every post aligns with your brand's goals and audience interests, ultimately driving your real estate business growth on Instagram.

Page 11: Creating a Content Calendar for Consistency

Consistency is key to building a strong presence on Instagram, and a well-planned **content calendar** is your best tool to stay organized and on track. Posting regularly keeps your audience engaged, boosts your visibility, and signals the Instagram algorithm that your account is active.

Start by deciding **how often** you want to post. For real estate, a good baseline is **3-5 posts per week**, combined with daily stories and weekly reels or live sessions. This frequency keeps your audience informed without overwhelming them.

Next, map out your **content pillars** (as we discussed earlier) across the calendar. For example:

- Monday: Property showcase
- Wednesday: Educational post
- Friday: Client testimonial
- Saturday: Community spotlight
- Sunday: Behind-the-scenes or Q&A

Use tools like **Google Sheets, Trello, or dedicated apps like Later, Buffer** to create and manage your calendar. These platforms also let you schedule posts ahead of time, saving you daily effort.

Include important dates like holidays, industry events, or local festivals. Tailor your content around these to stay relevant and timely. For example, a post about "Best

Neighbourhoods for Families" during school admission season.

Plan your captions, hashtags, and CTAs in advance to maintain quality and engagement. Don't forget to allocate time for **engagement**—replying to comments and DMs.

Review your calendar weekly or monthly to analyse performance and adjust content types or posting frequency based on insights. Flexibility is important, but structure prevents chaos.

In summary, a content calendar is your roadmap to consistent, strategic Instagram marketing. It saves time, reduces stress, and ensures your real estate brand grows steadily and effectively.

Page 12: Crafting Captivating Captions

Captions are more than just descriptions—they're your opportunity to tell stories, connect emotionally, and drive action on Instagram. A captivating caption can turn a casual scroller into a loyal follower or even a client.

Start your caption with a **hook** that grabs attention within the first two lines. This could be a bold statement, question, or interesting fact related to your real estate post. For example: "Did you know 70% of home buyers regret skipping a home inspection?"

Next, provide **value** by sharing useful information, a story, or insight. For real estate, you might explain a listing's unique features, give tips for buyers, or share a client success story.

Keep your tone **authentic and relatable**—avoid sounding overly salesy. Use simple language and inject your personality to build trust.

Encourage **engagement** by asking questions or inviting followers to share their opinions, experiences, or tag friends. Examples:
"What's your must-have home feature?"
"Tag someone who's house hunting!"

Use **line breaks and emojis** to make the caption easier to read and visually appealing.

Always include a clear **call to action (CTA)** that tells followers what you want them to do next:
"DM us for a free consultation!"

"Click the link in bio to view listings."
"Save this post for your home buying checklist."

Finally, consider using **hashtags** within or after the caption to increase reach and discoverability. Target local and niche hashtags relevant to real estate.

Remember, captions extend the story your photo or video starts. Craft them thoughtfully to inspire, educate, and convert your audience into engaged followers and clients.

Page 13: Effective Use of Hashtags

Hashtags are one of Instagram's most powerful tools for expanding your reach and attracting new followers, especially in the competitive real estate market. When used strategically, hashtags help your posts get discovered by people interested in your services, increasing visibility and engagement.

Start by researching relevant hashtags related to your niche, location, and audience. For real estate, mix three types of hashtags:

1. **Broad hashtags** (e.g., #RealEstate, #PropertyForSale) – High competition but large audience.

2. **Niche-specific hashtags** (e.g., #MumbaiHomes, #LuxuryRealEstateIndia) – More targeted with engaged users.

3. **Branded hashtags** (e.g., #ElitePropertyHub, #AnkitRealtyTips) – Unique to your business and help build brand identity.

Use a combination of **10 to 30 hashtags** per post. Instagram allows up to 30, but quality over quantity is key. Avoid irrelevant or banned hashtags, as they can reduce your post's reach.

Place hashtags either at the **end of your caption** or in the **first comment** to keep your post clean and visually appealing.

Use **location-based hashtags** frequently, such as the neighbourhood or city where your properties are located (#BandraFlats, #DelhiRealEstate). This targets local buyers and investors actively searching for options in those areas.

Create a **hashtag bank** with groups of hashtags that work well for different content pillars (listings, tips, testimonials). Rotate these groups to avoid repetition and reach different audiences.

Regularly review hashtag performance through Instagram Insights to identify which ones drive the most impressions and engagement, then refine your strategy accordingly.

In summary, smart hashtag use increases your content's discoverability and attracts the right audience to your real estate Instagram page, helping you grow your business faster.

Page 14: Leveraging Instagram Stories for Engagement

Instagram Stories are a dynamic and highly engaging way to connect with your audience in real-time. Stories appear at the top of the Instagram feed, offering prime visibility and a more casual, authentic way to showcase your real estate business.

Use Stories to share behind-the-scenes glimpses of property tours, office life, or your daily routine. This builds trust and relatability, helping followers feel more connected to your brand.

Interactive features like **polls, quizzes, question stickers, and countdowns** encourage direct engagement. For example, run a poll asking, "Which kitchen style do you prefer?" or use the question sticker to answer followers' real estate questions live.

Stories also allow you to post **time-sensitive content** such as limited-time offers, open house announcements, or market updates. Use the countdown sticker to build anticipation for upcoming events or launches.

Don't forget to use **location tags and hashtags** in your Stories to increase discoverability by local audiences. You can add multiple hashtags and a location sticker discreetly by minimizing their size or hiding them behind GIFs or stickers.

Another great tip: **Save your best Stories as Highlights** on your profile. Organize Highlights into categories like "Listings," "Buyer Tips," or "Client Reviews." This creates a valuable resource for new visitors to quickly learn about your services.

Keep your Stories consistent—aim to post daily or at least several times a week. This maintains top-of-mind awareness and helps build a loyal, engaged community.

In short, Instagram Stories are a powerful tool to showcase personality, educate your audience, and drive engagement—all essential for growing your real estate business on Instagram.

Page 15: Creating Eye-Catching Reels

Instagram Reels have become the platform's most powerful tool for organic reach and engagement. For real estate businesses, Reels offer an exciting way to showcase properties, share tips, and connect with a broader audience through short, dynamic videos.

Start your Reel with a **strong hook** in the first 3 seconds to capture attention. This could be a stunning property view, a surprising fact about real estate, or a quick teaser of what's coming.

Keep your content **concise and engaging**—Reels can be up to 90 seconds, but often 15-30 seconds works best. Use quick cuts, smooth transitions, and add text overlays to highlight key points or features.

Use **trending audio or music** to boost discoverability. Instagram favors Reels that use popular sounds and creative effects, so browse the Reels tab to spot trends and adapt them to your niche.

Popular Reel ideas for real estate include:

- Property walkthroughs highlighting unique features
- Quick tips for buyers and sellers
- Market updates and news bites
- Client testimonials or success stories
- Day-in-the-life glimpses of real estate agents

Add relevant **hashtags and location tags** to increase reach. Make sure your Reel's cover image is attractive and matches your brand aesthetics—this is what users see in your profile grid and on the Explore page.

Don't forget to include a clear **call to action** in your caption or video, like "DM us to schedule a tour!" or "Follow for daily real estate tips."

Consistency is key—posting Reels regularly can significantly grow your follower base and attract new leads by putting your content in front of interested viewers.

Page 16: Using Instagram Live to Build Trust

Instagram Live is an invaluable tool for real estate professionals looking to build authentic connections and trust with their audience. Unlike regular posts or stories, live videos allow real-time interaction, making your followers feel directly involved and valued.

Use Instagram Live to host **Q&A sessions** where you answer common questions about buying, selling, or financing property. This demonstrates your expertise and willingness to help, which builds credibility.

You can also do **virtual open houses** or live property tours, giving viewers an immersive experience. Encourage viewers to ask questions during the live stream, making it interactive and engaging.

Another effective use of Live is to **interview industry experts** such as mortgage brokers, interior designers, or legal advisors. This provides valuable insights and broadens your content appeal.

Promote your live sessions in advance through posts and stories to maximize attendance. Engage actively during the live by greeting viewers by name, responding to comments, and asking for their opinions.

After your session, save the video to your profile so followers who missed it can watch later. You can also repurpose clips for reels or stories.

Live videos show your personality and approachability, which is vital in real estate where trust is key to conversions. Regularly going live keeps your audience engaged, informed, and connected.

In summary, Instagram Live offers a powerful way to humanize your brand, answer questions on the spot, and build lasting relationships that drive real estate growth.

Page 17: Collaborations and Influencer Marketing on Instagram

Collaborations and influencer marketing can significantly boost your real estate business's visibility and credibility on Instagram. Partnering with influencers or complementary brands allows you to tap into their established audiences and gain trust faster.

Start by identifying **local influencers** or micro-influencers in related niches such as home décor, lifestyle, finance, or local community pages. Look for influencers with authentic engagement, not just follower counts.

Collaborations can take many forms:

- **Co-host Instagram Lives or Reels** discussing real estate trends or home buying tips

- Have influencers **tour your properties** and share honest reviews

- Run **giveaways or contests** together to increase reach and engagement

- Feature influencers as guest speakers in your stories or posts

Partnering with complementary businesses like mortgage brokers, interior designers, or moving companies for cross-promotions can also expand your network and add value to your followers.

When approaching influencers, be clear about the goals, deliverables, and compensation, whether it's payment, free services, or mutual promotion. Authenticity is key—choose partners who genuinely align with your brand and audience.

Collaborations increase trust, diversify your content, and attract new followers who are already interested in your industry, helping your real estate business grow organically and sustainably on Instagram.

Page 18: Running Instagram Ads for Real Estate

Instagram Ads offer powerful tools to reach a highly targeted audience quickly, making them essential for scaling your real estate business. Unlike organic posts, ads can be tailored to specific demographics, interests, and behaviours, ensuring your message reaches potential buyers or sellers actively looking for properties.

Start by defining your **campaign objective**—whether it's increasing brand awareness, generating leads, or driving website traffic. Instagram Ads integrate with Facebook's Ads Manager, providing robust targeting options such as location, age, income, interests, and behaviours.

For real estate, use eye-catching visuals or videos of properties combined with clear, compelling calls to action like "Schedule a Viewing," "Download Our Buyer's Guide," or "Contact Us Today."

Experiment with different ad formats:

- **Photo Ads** to highlight beautiful property images
- **Video Ads** or Reels to offer virtual tours or testimonials
- **Carousel Ads** to showcase multiple listings or features
- **Story Ads** for time-sensitive promotions or announcements

Set a budget that fits your goals and test multiple ad variations to see what resonates best. Monitor key metrics like impressions, click-through rates, and lead conversions to optimize your campaigns.

Remember to link your ads to dedicated landing pages or contact forms to capture leads efficiently.

In conclusion, Instagram Ads are a cost-effective way to accelerate your real estate marketing, allowing you to reach motivated buyers and grow your business faster.

Page 19: Optimizing Your Instagram Profile for Business

Your Instagram profile is often the first impression potential clients get of your real estate business. Optimizing it effectively ensures visitors understand who you are, what you offer, and how to connect with you—turning browsers into followers and leads.

Start with a **clear and professional profile photo**, ideally your business logo or a high-quality headshot if you're a personal brand. This builds trust and brand recognition.

Your **username and display name** should be easy to remember and include relevant keywords like your location or industry, for example, @MumbaiHomeExperts.

Craft a compelling **bio** that explains what you do and who you serve in 150 characters or less. Use keywords such as "Real Estate," "Property Sales," or "Luxury Homes" to improve searchability. Include a **call to action (CTA)** like "DM for listings" or "Book a free consultation."

Utilize the **website link** strategically. Link to your real estate website, a landing page for lead capture, or a Linktree with multiple important links (listings, contact, resources).

Make use of **Instagram Story Highlights** to showcase important categories such as "Listings," "Client Reviews," "FAQs," or "Market Updates." Use consistent highlight covers for a polished look.

Lastly, switch your account to a **Business or Creator profile** to access Instagram Insights, ads, and contact buttons, making it easier for potential clients to reach you via call, email, or message.

An optimized profile clearly communicates your brand, builds credibility, and simplifies the path for visitors to engage and convert into clients.

Page 20: Using Instagram Analytics to Improve Your Strategy

Instagram Analytics, available through Instagram Insights on Business accounts, is a vital tool for understanding what's working and where to improve in your real estate marketing efforts. Tracking your data helps you make informed decisions that boost engagement, reach, and conversions.

Start by regularly reviewing key metrics such as:

- **Impressions and Reach:** How many people see your posts and stories? This shows the visibility of your content.

- **Engagement:** Likes, comments, shares, saves, and story interactions indicate how well your content resonates with your audience.

- **Follower Growth:** Track how your follower count changes over time to measure overall brand growth.

- **Profile Visits and Website Clicks:** These actions show how effectively your profile and CTAs drive traffic to your business.

Analyse which posts perform best. Look for patterns in content type, timing, captions, and hashtags. For instance, do video tours get more saves? Do educational posts spark more comments? Use these insights to refine your content strategy.

Pay attention to your audience demographics—age, gender, location, and active hours—to tailor your content and posting schedule for maximum impact.

Don't forget to evaluate your Instagram Stories and Reels separately since they have unique analytics like forward taps, exits, and replies. This helps identify the most engaging formats and topics.

Set monthly goals based on your analytics and test new strategies, measuring results to continuously optimize your approach.

In short, Instagram Analytics provides the feedback loop you need to sharpen your real estate marketing tactics, ensuring you invest your time and resources where they yield the highest returns.

Page 21: Building Relationships Through Instagram Engagement

Instagram engagement goes beyond likes and follows—it's about creating meaningful interactions that build trust and long-term relationships with your audience. For real estate, these relationships can translate into referrals, repeat business, and strong brand loyalty.

Start by responding promptly to comments and direct messages. Show genuine interest in your followers' questions or concerns, whether they're about a listing or market advice. Personalized replies make your audience feel valued.

Engage proactively by liking and commenting on posts from your target audience, local businesses, or industry partners. This helps you get noticed and builds community.

Use Instagram's interactive features like polls, quizzes, and question stickers in Stories to encourage two-way communication. For example, ask followers about their home preferences or invite them to submit real estate questions.

Create posts that invite conversation—pose questions, ask for opinions, or run contests that require comments and tagging friends. The more engagement your posts receive, the higher their visibility due to Instagram's algorithm.

Host giveaways or referral programs to reward your followers for spreading the word about your business.

Remember, consistent, authentic engagement fosters trust and positions you as a helpful, approachable expert in real estate.

Building these relationships over time turns your Instagram followers into clients and advocates, fuelling sustainable business growth.

42

Page 22: Storytelling Techniques to Connect with Your Audience

Storytelling is a powerful way to engage your Instagram audience emotionally, making your real estate brand memorable and relatable. People remember stories more than facts or sales pitches, so weaving narratives into your posts can deepen connections and drive action.

Start by sharing **client success stories**—how you helped a family find their dream home or assisted a seller in getting the best deal. Use before-and-after images or short videos to illustrate the journey.

Showcase your own **behind-the-scenes** experiences: property scouting, negotiations, or team celebrations. This humanizes your brand and builds trust.

Use the classic story structure: **beginning, middle, and end.** For example, introduce a challenge a client faced, explain how you helped overcome it, and share the positive outcome.

Incorporate **emotions and sensory details** to make your stories vivid. Describe the excitement of moving into a new neighbourhood or the peace of a quiet balcony view.

Use **Instagram Stories and Reels** for quick, engaging storytelling formats. You can create mini-series or episodic content like "Home Buying Tips" or "Neighbourhood Spotlights."

Ask your audience to share their stories or experiences related to real estate, creating a two-way conversation.

Effective storytelling builds empathy, trust, and a deeper relationship with your followers—turning them into loyal clients and advocates for your real estate business.

Page 23: Leveraging User-Generated Content (UGC)

User-Generated Content (UGC) refers to any content your followers, clients, or fans create about your real estate business and share on Instagram. Leveraging UGC can be a game-changer for building trust and authenticity because potential clients see real people's experiences, not just polished marketing.

Encourage clients to share photos or videos of their new homes, renovations, or testimonials and tag your account. You can also create branded hashtags (e.g., #HappyHomeownersWith[YourBrand]) to collect and showcase their content easily.

Reposting UGC on your profile or stories provides social proof, showing that real people trust and appreciate your services. It also fills your feed with diverse, genuine content without extra effort.

To motivate followers, run contests or campaigns asking clients to share their stories or photos in exchange for a feature or small prize. Highlighting client experiences creates a positive community vibe.

Always ask permission before sharing UGC and credit the original creator to maintain trust and goodwill.

Integrating UGC strengthens your brand's credibility, expands your reach as users' networks see your content, and nurtures a loyal, engaged community—essential ingredients for real estate business growth on Instagram.

Page 24: Using Instagram Guides to Showcase Neighbourhoods and Listings

Instagram Guides are a versatile content format that lets you curate posts, places, or product recommendations into a single, scrollable resource. For real estate professionals, Guides provide an excellent way to organize and showcase neighbourhoods, listings, and helpful tips in one place.

Create a **Neighbourhood Guide** featuring posts about local amenities, schools, parks, restaurants, and transportation options. This helps potential buyers understand the lifestyle and benefits of living in that area, making your listings more appealing.

You can also make **Listing Guides** that highlight your current properties, grouped by price range, type (apartments, villas), or location. Each listing can include photos, videos, and key details to provide a comprehensive overview.

Additionally, offer **Educational Guides** on topics like the home buying process, financing tips, or property maintenance. These guides position you as a knowledgeable resource and help build trust with your audience.

Guides are easy to share and promote in your stories, posts, or even your bio link, driving traffic and engagement.

By using Instagram Guides effectively, you give your followers a rich, organized experience that can simplify their decision-making process and position you as a go-to real estate expert.

Page 25: Instagram Content Planning and Scheduling

Consistency is key to success on Instagram, especially in the competitive real estate market. Having a well-organized content plan and schedule ensures you post regularly, maintain engagement, and cover all essential topics without scrambling for ideas.

Start by defining your **content pillars**—the main themes you want to focus on. For real estate, these might include:

- Property listings and virtual tours

- Market updates and news

- Client testimonials and success stories

- Educational content like buying/selling tips

- Behind-the-scenes glimpses

- Community and neighbourhood highlights

Create a **content calendar** that maps out what you will post and when. Use tools like Google Sheets, Trello, or specialized apps like Later, Buffer, or Hootsuite to plan ahead. Aim for a mix of post types (photos, videos, reels, stories) to keep your feed dynamic.

Consider the best **posting times** based on your audience's activity, usually mornings, lunch hours, or evenings.

Batch-create content in advance to save time and reduce last-minute pressure. For example, schedule a photo shoot day or record several reels in one go.

Track what works through engagement and analytics, then tweak your calendar accordingly.

Planning and scheduling your Instagram content ensures you stay consistent, relevant, and organized—helping your real estate business grow steadily and professionally.

Page 26: Crafting Compelling Captions That Convert

Captions are your opportunity to tell a story, share valuable information, and inspire action—making them a critical part of your Instagram real estate strategy. A well-crafted caption can transform casual scrollers into engaged followers and clients.

Start with a **hook** that grabs attention within the first few words. Ask a question, share a surprising fact, or make a bold statement related to the property or real estate market.

Use a **conversational tone** that reflects your brand's personality. Be authentic and approachable, as if you're talking to a friend or client face-to-face.

Provide **useful information** like key property features, neighbourhood benefits, or market insights. Highlight what makes the listing unique or why now is the perfect time to buy or sell.

Incorporate **emojis** and line breaks to make captions easier to read and visually appealing.

Always include a **call to action (CTA)** that guides your audience on the next step, such as "DM us for a private tour," "Comment your favourite feature," or "Click the link in bio to learn more."

Keep SEO in mind by including relevant keywords and hashtags naturally within the caption.

Test different styles and lengths to see what resonates best with your audience and drives the most engagement.

In summary, compelling captions engage your audience emotionally and logically, motivating them to interact and take action, which ultimately helps grow your real estate business on Instagram.

Page 27: Hashtag Strategies for Maximum Reach

Hashtags are essential on Instagram to increase your content's visibility and attract the right audience. For real estate businesses, using the right hashtags helps you connect with potential buyers, sellers, and local communities.

Start by researching **relevant hashtags** related to your niche, location, and audience. Combine broad hashtags like #RealEstate, #HomeForSale, or #Property with more specific ones such as #NYCRealEstate, #LuxuryHomesLA, or #FirstTimeHomeBuyer.

Use a mix of:

- **Popular hashtags** with millions of posts to gain broader exposure

- **Niche-specific hashtags** that directly target real estate audiences

- **Local hashtags** that focus on your city, neighbourhood, or region (e.g., #DallasHomes, #BrooklynLiving)

Instagram allows up to 30 hashtags per post, but studies show 9 to 15 relevant hashtags often perform best without looking spammy.

Create a **branded hashtag** unique to your business, like #[YourBusinessName]Homes, and encourage clients and followers to use it when posting about their experiences with you.

Place hashtags either in the caption or in the first comment to keep your post looking clean.

Regularly update your hashtag list based on performance and trends. Use Instagram Insights or third-party tools to track which hashtags drive the most engagement.

Effective hashtag strategies help expand your reach, increase post discovery, and grow your real estate audience organically.

Page 28: Engaging with Your Local Community on Instagram

Engaging with your local community on Instagram is vital for real estate professionals because buying a home is deeply tied to location and neighbourhood vibes. Building strong local connections boosts your reputation, trust, and leads.

Start by **following local businesses, influencers, and community groups** on Instagram. Engage with their content by liking, commenting, and sharing relevant posts. This builds goodwill and visibility within your area.

Share **content that highlights your community**—local events, festivals, restaurants, parks, schools, or infrastructure developments. Showcasing these aspects helps potential buyers envision life in the neighbourhood.

Use **location tags and local hashtags** consistently to reach people interested in your area. For example, tagging #DenverHomes or #SeattleNeighborhoods targets local users.

Host or promote **community events** such as open houses, charity drives, or neighbourhood cleanups through your Instagram stories and posts to foster relationships and position yourself as a community leader.

Collaborate with local businesses for giveaways or cross-promotions, exposing your brand to a broader, relevant audience.

Respond to comments and DMs quickly, demonstrating your commitment to helping locals with their real estate needs.

In summary, genuine local engagement creates a loyal, connected audience that is more likely to trust and choose you when it's time to buy or sell.

56

Page 29: Using Instagram Stories Highlights to Showcase Your Expertise

Instagram Stories Highlights are a powerful way to keep your best content visible beyond the usual 24-hour limit. For real estate professionals, Highlights serve as a mini portfolio, showcasing your expertise, services, and personality all in one place.

Create Highlights based on key themes such as:

- **Property Tours:** Showcasing your current and past listings with video walkthroughs or photos.

- **Client Testimonials:** Featuring positive reviews and success stories to build trust.

- **Market Tips:** Sharing quick advice on buying, selling, or financing homes.

- **Neighbourhood Spotlights:** Highlighting local amenities, schools, and lifestyle to attract buyers.

- **Behind the Scenes:** Offering a peek into your daily work, team, or events to humanize your brand.

Use **custom Highlight covers** with consistent branding and colours to maintain a polished, professional look.

Keep Highlights updated by adding fresh stories and archiving outdated ones. This ensures your profile always reflects your latest offerings and knowledge.

Guide visitors to explore these Highlights in your bio or posts, as they offer a quick way to learn about your business without scrolling through your entire feed.

In essence, Stories Highlights function as a dynamic, evergreen resource that educates, builds credibility, and nurtures trust with your Instagram audience—key for converting followers into clients.

Page 30: Creating Engaging Instagram Reels for Real Estate

Instagram Reels have rapidly become one of the most popular content formats on the platform, offering a fantastic opportunity for real estate professionals to showcase properties and engage with potential clients in a dynamic way.

Reels are short, entertaining videos (up to 90 seconds) that can highlight property tours, neighbourhood features, or quick tips. Their algorithm favors Reels, often giving them more visibility than regular posts, which means greater organic reach.

To create engaging Reels, start with a strong **hook**—capture attention within the first few seconds by showing a stunning view or intriguing fact. Use trending music or sounds to boost discoverability, but ensure they align with your brand's tone.

Keep content **informative and visually appealing**: highlight unique property features, show before-and-after transformations, or give quick market updates. Use captions and stickers to emphasize key points.

Don't hesitate to inject personality and authenticity—people connect with real estate agents who feel approachable and genuine.

Add a clear **call to action** like "Contact us for a private tour" or "Follow for more real estate tips."

Post Reels consistently to build momentum and experiment with different formats, such as "Day in the Life," client testimonials, or FAQs.

By leveraging Instagram Reels creatively, you can capture attention, grow your audience, and generate high-quality leads for your real estate business.

Page 31: Instagram Live: Real-Time Engagement and Q&A

Instagram Live is a powerful tool for real estate professionals to connect with their audience in real time, build trust, and answer questions directly. It allows you to showcase your expertise, highlight listings, and engage with potential clients more personally.

Plan your live sessions around topics your audience cares about, such as virtual property tours, market updates, buying/selling tips, or answering frequently asked questions.

Promote your Instagram Live in advance through stories, posts, and countdown stickers to maximize attendance.

During the live session, interact with viewers by answering their questions, addressing comments, and calling out participants by name to create a personal connection.

Use Instagram Live to invite guest experts, such as mortgage brokers, home inspectors, or satisfied clients, adding credibility and varied perspectives.

Save your live videos to your Stories Highlights so followers who missed the session can watch later.

Regular Instagram Live sessions help you establish authority, nurture relationships, and encourage immediate action, such as booking a consultation or visiting an open house.

Incorporate Live into your Instagram marketing mix to deepen engagement and accelerate your real estate business growth.

62

Page 32: Collaborating with Influencers and Partners on Instagram

Collaborating with influencers and local partners on Instagram can significantly expand your reach and credibility in the real estate market. Influencers have loyal audiences that trust their opinions, making their endorsements powerful for your business.

Start by identifying **micro-influencers**—those with smaller but highly engaged followers in your niche or local area. For real estate, this might include local lifestyle bloggers, interior designers, or community figures.

Propose mutually beneficial collaborations such as:

- Sponsored posts or stories featuring your listings

- Joint giveaways or contests to attract new followers

- Co-hosted Instagram Lives discussing home buying tips or market trends

- Featuring influencers as guests during open houses or virtual tours

Partnering with local businesses like moving companies, furniture stores, or mortgage brokers can also create cross-promotional opportunities. Tag each other in posts and stories to tap into each other's audiences.

Maintain clear communication and set expectations regarding content, timing, and goals to ensure a smooth collaboration.

Collaborations help build your brand's authenticity, reach new potential clients, and add variety to your Instagram content.

By leveraging the networks of trusted influencers and partners, you can grow your real estate business faster and stronger on Instagram.

Page 33: Running Instagram Ads for Real Estate Success

Instagram Ads are a powerful way to reach a highly targeted audience and generate quality leads for your real estate business. Unlike organic posts, ads let you tailor your message to specific demographics, locations, and interests.

Start by setting clear goals: Are you promoting a new listing, driving traffic to your website, or increasing brand awareness? Your objectives will guide your ad format and messaging.

Choose the right ad type for your campaign:

- **Photo Ads** to showcase stunning property images
- **Video Ads** for virtual tours or client testimonials
- **Carousel Ads** to display multiple listings or features
- **Story Ads** for immersive, full-screen experiences with quick calls to action

Use Instagram's **targeting tools** to narrow your audience by location (city, neighbourhood), age, income, interests (home buying, interior design), and behaviours.

Craft compelling ad copy and include a strong **call to action** such as "Schedule a Viewing," "Contact Us," or "Learn More."

Set a budget and duration that fit your goals, and monitor performance through Instagram Ads Manager to optimize for better results.

Test different creatives and audience segments to identify what works best, and continually refine your ads.

Instagram Ads amplify your reach, accelerate lead generation, and drive measurable growth for your real estate business.

Page 34: Optimizing Your Instagram Profile for Business

Your Instagram profile is often the first impression potential clients get of your real estate business. Optimizing it effectively can increase trust, drive engagement, and convert visitors into followers or leads.

Start with a **clear and professional profile photo**, such as your logo or a high-quality headshot. This builds brand recognition and credibility.

Craft a **compelling bio** that succinctly explains what you do, who you serve, and what makes you unique. Include keywords like "Real Estate Agent," "Home Buying Expert," or your location to improve discoverability.

Use a **call-to-action (CTA)** in your bio, such as "DM for listings" or "Click below to schedule a consultation," paired with a link to your website, booking page, or a lead capture tool.

Leverage Instagram's **Contact Buttons** (Call, Email, Directions) to make it easy for followers to get in touch directly from your profile.

Utilize the **Story Highlights** feature to showcase important content like testimonials, listings, FAQs, and neighbourhood tours, providing visitors instant access to your expertise.

Keep your **username and display name simple and searchable**, ideally including your business name or location.

Regularly update your profile to reflect new services, achievements, or promotions.

A well-optimized Instagram profile acts as a powerful business card, welcoming potential clients and encouraging them to take the next step in their real estate journey.

Page 35: Measuring Instagram Analytics to Improve Your Strategy

To grow your real estate business on Instagram effectively, you must track and analyse your performance regularly. Instagram Analytics, also known as Insights, provides valuable data to understand what content resonates with your audience and how to refine your strategy.

Key metrics to monitor include:

- **Impressions & Reach:** How many times your posts are seen and how many unique users view them.

- **Engagement Rate:** Likes, comments, shares, and saves relative to your follower count—indicating how engaging your content is.

- **Follower Growth:** Tracks how your audience size changes over time.

- **Website Clicks & Profile Visits:** Shows how well your profile drives traffic to your real estate website or landing pages.

- **Stories & Reels Metrics:** Views, exits, replies, and interactions to gauge short-form content effectiveness.

Use this data to identify your best-performing posts and understand what types of content (photos, videos, reels) and topics your audience prefers.

Test different posting times and formats, then analyse which generate the most engagement or leads.

Adjust your hashtag strategy based on reach and discovery metrics.

Regularly reviewing Instagram Analytics helps you make informed decisions, optimize your content, and ultimately accelerate your real estate business growth on the platform.

Page 36: Building a Consistent Brand Voice on Instagram

A consistent brand voice helps your real estate business stand out on Instagram and fosters a strong connection with your audience. It reflects your personality, values, and professionalism, making your content recognizable and trustworthy.

Start by defining your brand voice. Is it professional and authoritative, warm and friendly, or energetic and motivational? Your voice should align with your target audience's expectations and preferences.

Maintain this tone across all captions, stories, comments, and messages. For example, if your voice is friendly and approachable, avoid overly formal language or jargon. If authoritative, back your claims with data and market expertise.

Use consistent vocabulary, phrases, and storytelling style. This familiarity helps followers connect emotionally and remember your brand.

Visual branding—colours, fonts, logo—also supports your voice, creating a cohesive look and feel on your profile.

A clear, consistent brand voice builds trust, encourages engagement, and strengthens your real estate business's identity on Instagram.

Page 37: Utilizing Instagram DM for Lead Nurturing

Direct Messages (DMs) on Instagram offer a private, personal channel to nurture leads and build relationships with potential real estate clients. Effective use of DMs can convert casual followers into serious buyers or sellers.

Start by responding promptly and warmly to all inquiries, comments, and story replies. Quick engagement shows professionalism and attentiveness.

Use DMs to provide personalized information, such as sending property details, scheduling tours, or answering specific questions about listings and the buying process.

Leverage automated welcome messages or quick replies for common questions to save time, but always personalize follow-ups.

Segment your DM conversations by interest or stage in the buying cycle—first-time buyers, investors, sellers—and tailor your communication accordingly.

Share exclusive offers or sneak peeks of upcoming listings via DM to create a sense of VIP treatment.

Respect privacy and avoid spamming; focus on building genuine connections and trust.

By mastering Instagram DMs, you create meaningful conversations that guide prospects smoothly through their real estate journey, boosting your chances of closing deals.

Page 38: Leveraging User-Generated Content for Trust and Reach

User-generated content (UGC) is any content your clients or followers create about your real estate business, such as photos, videos, testimonials, or reviews. Leveraging UGC on Instagram is a powerful way to build trust and expand your reach authentically.

Encourage satisfied clients to share their home-buying or selling experience by tagging your account or using your branded hashtag. This creates authentic social proof that resonates more deeply than branded posts.

Repost client testimonials, before-and-after photos, or user-shared moments of moving into their new home. Always ask permission and credit the original creator.

Run contests or campaigns inviting followers to share their favourite home features or renovation stories, increasing engagement and UGC volume.

UGC enhances your content variety and builds a community feeling, showing prospective client's real stories and positive outcomes.

It also signals to Instagram's algorithm that your brand is engaging and trustworthy, which can improve your content's visibility.

Incorporate UGC regularly to humanize your brand, strengthen relationships, and attract more qualified leads for your real estate business.

Page 39: Using Instagram Insights to Understand Your Audience

Understanding your audience is crucial for creating content that resonates and drives engagement on Instagram. Instagram Insights provides detailed data about your followers' demographics, behaviours, and preferences, helping you tailor your real estate marketing effectively.

Start by analysing **follower demographics**: age, gender, location, and active hours. Knowing where your audience lives and when they're online allows you to post content at optimal times and focus on the right neighbourhoods or cities.

Check **content performance metrics** like likes, comments, saves, and shares to see which posts or stories your audience prefers. Notice if videos, photos, or reels perform better and create more of that content.

Explore **engagement patterns** to identify what topics interest your audience most—property tours, market tips, neighbourhood highlights, or client stories.

Monitor **growth trends** to understand which strategies or campaigns attract new followers.

Use this data to refine your content calendar, adjust your messaging, and improve targeting in both organic posts and paid ads.

By leveraging Instagram Insights, you can create more relevant, impactful content that attracts and retains potential real estate clients.

Page 40: Crafting Your Instagram Content Calendar

A well-planned content calendar keeps your Instagram marketing organized, consistent, and strategic—key factors for growing your real estate business.

Start by deciding how often you'll post, balancing quality and quantity. For real estate, aim for 3-5 posts per week plus regular stories and reels.

Identify key content pillars that align with your goals and audience interests, such as:

- Property listings and tours

- Market insights and tips

- Client testimonials and success stories

- Neighbourhood features and community events

- Behind-the-scenes glimpses of your work

Map out themes and topics weekly or monthly, mixing formats like photos, videos, carousels, reels, and live sessions to keep your feed dynamic.

Schedule posts around important dates like holidays, local events, or real estate seasons (e.g., spring buying season).

Use planning tools like Later, Buffer, or Hootsuite to schedule posts in advance, ensuring consistency even during busy times.

Review performance monthly and adjust your calendar based on what content drives the most engagement and leads.

A strategic content calendar ensures your Instagram presence is professional, engaging, and focused on converting followers into clients.

Page 41: Instagram Bio Optimization for Real Estate Professionals

Your Instagram bio is the first impression visitors get of your real estate business. Optimizing it effectively can increase profile visits, followers, and leads.

Start with a clear, concise description of what you do and who you serve. Use keywords like "Real Estate Agent," "Home Buyer Specialist," or "Luxury Properties" to improve searchability.

Highlight your unique selling points or specialties, such as "Helping first-time buyers" or "Expert in downtown condos."

Incorporate a call-to-action (CTA) that guides visitors on what to do next—examples include "DM for listings," "Schedule a consultation," or "Click link below for free home evaluation."

Add a link to your website, lead capture form, or property listings using a link service like Linktree if you want to share multiple URLs.

Include contact options like email, phone, or directions via Instagram's business profile features for easy access.

Use emojis sparingly to add personality and break up text for readability.

Keep your bio updated to reflect new offers, achievements, or services.

A strong bio builds trust and encourages potential clients to connect with you, driving your real estate business growth.

Page 42: Creating Engaging Captions That Convert

Captions are your chance to tell a story, connect emotionally, and motivate action on Instagram. For real estate, effective captions can turn casual scrollers into serious clients.

Start with a **hook** that grabs attention — ask a question, share an interesting fact, or spark curiosity. For example, "Looking for your dream home in [City]? Here's why this listing stands out!"

Be **authentic and relatable**—share client success stories, challenges, or your passion for helping buyers and sellers.

Use **clear calls to action (CTAs)** like "DM me for a private tour," "Comment your favorite feature," or "Click the link in bio to learn more."

Incorporate **emojis** to break text and add personality, but don't overdo it.

Keep captions **concise but informative**—too long might lose attention, too short might miss context.

End with a question or invitation to engage, encouraging likes, comments, or shares.

Finally, tailor your captions to your target audience's language and preferences for stronger connection.

Well-crafted captions boost engagement, build trust, and drive leads for your real estate business on Instagram.

Page 43: Using Hashtags Effectively on Instagram

Hashtags are essential for increasing your real estate content's visibility on Instagram. When used strategically, they help you reach a wider, targeted audience beyond your current followers.

Start by researching relevant hashtags related to real estate, your location, and your niche—such as #RealEstateAgent, #DreamHome, #CityNameHomes, #FirstTimeBuyer, or #LuxuryRealEstate.

Mix **popular, moderate, and niche hashtags** to maximize reach without getting lost in overly saturated tags. For example, combine #RealEstate (very popular) with #CityNameRealEstate (moderate) and #CityNeighborhoodHomes (niche).

Use up to 30 hashtags per post, but quality matters more than quantity. Avoid irrelevant or banned hashtags to prevent shadow banning.

Create a **branded hashtag** unique to your business (e.g., #YourNameRealty) to encourage followers and clients to tag you in their posts, building community and user-generated content.

Place hashtags either in the caption or the first comment to keep posts visually clean.

Regularly review hashtag performance using Instagram Insights to find which tags bring the most engagement and adjust your strategy accordingly.

Effectively using hashtags can boost your content's discoverability, attract targeted leads, and accelerate your real estate business growth on Instagram.

Page 44: Instagram Stories Ideas for Real Estate Engagement

Instagram Stories are a dynamic way to connect with your audience daily, offering behind-the-scenes glimpses and quick, engaging updates that build relationships and trust.

Here are some creative Story ideas for real estate:

- **Property Tours:** Share short clips or walkthroughs of new listings or open houses.

- **Client Testimonials:** Post video or text testimonials from happy clients.

- **Polls and Questions:** Use interactive stickers to ask followers about their dream home features or answer real estate FAQs.

- **Market Updates:** Share quick updates on local market trends or mortgage rates.

- **Before-and-After:** Show renovation projects or staging transformations.

- **Day in the Life:** Let followers see your daily routine as a real estate agent.

- **Exclusive Sneak Peeks:** Offer first looks at upcoming listings or special deals.

- **Local Highlights:** Showcase nearby amenities, parks, restaurants, or community events.

Keep Stories authentic and conversational to foster engagement. Use relevant hashtags and location tags to increase discoverability.

Save important Stories in Highlights to provide ongoing value and easy access for new visitors.

Consistent, creative Story content keeps your audience engaged and increases the chances of converting followers into clients.

Page 45: Harnessing Instagram Reels for Real Estate Marketing

Instagram Reels are short, engaging videos that can dramatically increase your real estate business's reach and visibility. Their high priority in Instagram's algorithm makes them a powerful tool for attracting new followers and leads.

Create Reels showcasing:

- Quick property tours with dynamic shots
- Home buying or selling tips in bite-sized formats
- Client testimonials or success stories
- Neighbourhood highlights or community events
- Before-and-after transformations or staging tips

Use trending music and hashtags to boost discoverability. Keep Reels fun, informative, and visually appealing to capture attention quickly.

Consistency is key—post Reels regularly to stay relevant in your audience's feed.

Use calls to action such as "Follow for more tips" or "DM to schedule a viewing" to encourage engagement.

Analyse which types of Reels perform best and tailor your content accordingly.

By leveraging Instagram Reels, you can showcase your expertise, build trust, and attract more potential buyers and sellers.

Page 46: Collaborating with Local Businesses on Instagram

Collaborating with local businesses on Instagram can boost your real estate brand by tapping into complementary audiences and building community trust.

Start by identifying local businesses that share your target market, such as:

- Home staging companies
- Interior designers
- Mortgage brokers
- Moving services
- Furniture stores

Reach out for mutually beneficial partnerships like:

- Co-hosted Instagram Lives or giveaways
- Cross-promotional posts tagging each other
- Sharing exclusive offers or discounts for each other's followers

These collaborations expand your reach and add value to your audience, showing you're well-connected and supportive of the community.

Highlight local businesses in your content to position yourself as a neighbourhood expert.

Ensure all collaborations are authentic and align with your brand values.

By working with local businesses, you enhance your reputation and create a network that can drive referrals and new leads for your real estate business.

Page 47: Hosting Instagram Live Sessions to Engage Followers

Instagram Live offers a real-time, interactive way to connect with your audience, build trust, and showcase your expertise in the real estate market.

Plan your Live sessions around topics that interest your followers, such as:

- Market updates and trends

- Q&A sessions about buying or selling homes

- Virtual open houses or property walkthroughs

- Tips on home financing, staging, or renovations

- Interviews with local experts like mortgage brokers or interior designers

Promote your Live sessions in advance through posts and Stories to maximize attendance.

Engage with viewers by answering their questions and acknowledging comments during the broadcast to create a two-way conversation.

Save your Live videos to your Stories Highlights so followers can watch them later, extending their value.

Consistency in hosting Live sessions helps build a loyal community and positions you as a go-to real estate professional.

Use Instagram Live to humanize your brand and foster deeper connections, ultimately driving more leads and business growth.

Page 48: Using Instagram Highlights to Showcase Your Expertise

Instagram Highlights allow you to keep important Stories visible on your profile permanently, creating an organized showcase of your real estate expertise.

Create Highlights based on key categories, such as:

- **Listings:** Showcase current and past properties for sale.

- **Testimonials:** Share client reviews and success stories.

- **Neighbourhoods:** Highlight local amenities, schools, parks, and community vibes.

- **Tips & FAQs:** Offer advice on buying, selling, financing, and home maintenance.

- **Behind the Scenes:** Give followers a glimpse into your daily work and processes.

Use clear, branded cover images for each Highlight to maintain a professional and cohesive profile look.

Regularly update your Highlights to keep content fresh and relevant.

Highlights help new visitors quickly understand your services and expertise, boosting credibility and encouraging them to reach out.

Effectively curated Highlights turn your Instagram profile into a comprehensive portfolio that supports your real estate business growth.

Page 49: Engaging Your Audience with Instagram Polls and Quizzes

Instagram's interactive features like polls and quizzes are fantastic tools for engaging your real estate audience while gathering valuable insights.

Use **Polls** in Stories to ask simple yes/no or either/or questions related to home preferences, such as:

- "Do you prefer city living or suburbs?"

- "Which kitchen style do you like better?"

Polls encourage quick interaction and make your followers feel involved.

Quizzes let you test your audience's real estate knowledge or preferences, such as:

- "Guess the average home price in [Neighbourhood]!"

- "Which home feature adds the most value?"

Quizzes are fun and educational, boosting engagement and positioning you as a knowledgeable expert.

Use the feedback from polls and quizzes to tailor your content and services better to your audience's needs and interests.

These features foster a two-way conversation, build relationships, and increase your Instagram algorithm ranking, helping more potential clients find you.

Page 50: Instagram Ads for Targeted Real Estate Leads

Instagram Ads offer powerful targeting tools to reach the right audience for your real estate business, accelerating lead generation beyond organic reach.

Start by defining your ad goals—whether to increase website visits, generate inquiries, or boost open house attendance.

Use Facebook Ads Manager to create campaigns targeting demographics, locations, interests, behaviours, and even custom audiences based on your existing contacts.

Design eye-catching ads with high-quality photos or videos of your properties, compelling headlines, and clear calls to action like "Schedule a Tour" or "Contact Us Today."

Experiment with different formats:

- **Photo ads** to highlight beautiful listings

- **Video ads** for virtual tours or agent introductions

- **Carousel ads** to showcase multiple properties or features

Set a budget and monitor your ad performance regularly, adjusting targeting and creatives based on results.

Instagram Ads help you reach serious buyers and sellers, drive traffic to your listings, and grow your real estate business faster.

Page 51: Crafting Compelling Instagram Ad Copy

Creating engaging and persuasive ad copy is crucial to capturing attention and driving action on your Instagram real estate ads.

Start with a strong **headline** that addresses your audience's needs or desires. For example, "Find Your Dream Home in [City] Today!" or "Ready to Sell? Get Top Dollar Fast!"

Use concise, clear language focused on benefits—highlight what makes your property or service unique, such as "Spacious 3-bedroom with modern kitchen" or "Expert negotiation for highest price."

Include a clear **call-to-action (CTA)** that tells viewers exactly what to do next: "Book a Tour Now," "Contact Us Today," or "Learn More in Bio."

Keep the tone friendly and professional, aligning with your brand voice to build trust.

Use power words like "exclusive," "limited time," "new listing," or "just sold" to create urgency and excitement.

Test different versions of your copy (A/B testing) to find what resonates best with your target audience.

Strong ad copy paired with compelling visuals increases click-through rates and helps generate quality leads for your real estate business.

Page 52: Instagram Analytics for Optimizing Ad Campaigns

Instagram Analytics provides valuable data to help you track and improve the performance of your real estate ad campaigns.

Monitor key metrics such as:

- **Impressions** (how many times your ad was shown)

- **Reach** (unique users who saw your ad)

- **Engagement** (likes, comments, shares, saves)

- **Click-Through Rate (CTR)** (how many clicked your link or CTA)

- **Conversion Rate** (how many completed a desired action, like filling a form)

Analyse which ads are driving the best results and understand the demographics and behaviours of your most engaged audience segments.

Use this insight to tweak your targeting, adjust budgets, and refine your ad creative and copy for better ROI.

By consistently reviewing Instagram Analytics, you maximize your ad spend efficiency and attract more qualified leads for your real estate business.

Page 53: Building a Real Estate Brand on Instagram

Building a strong, recognizable brand on Instagram helps you stand out in a competitive real estate market and attract loyal clients.

Start by defining your brand identity: your mission, values, target audience, and unique selling proposition. Are you the expert in luxury homes, first-time buyers, or commercial real estate?

Maintain a consistent visual style—use a signature colour palette, fonts, and filters to create a cohesive look across your posts and Stories.

Craft a consistent voice in your captions and interactions—whether it's professional, friendly, or approachable—so followers know what to expect.

Share your story and behind-the-scenes content to humanize your brand and build emotional connections.

Use your logo and branded hashtag regularly to reinforce brand recognition.

Engage authentically with your audience by responding to comments and messages, building trust and relationships.

A strong Instagram brand increases credibility, fosters loyalty, and drives steady business growth over time.

Page 54: Instagram Networking Strategies for Real Estate Agents

Networking on Instagram is a powerful way to build relationships, increase referrals, and grow your real estate business.

Start by following and engaging with local businesses, community leaders, and industry professionals such as mortgage brokers, home inspectors, and interior designers.

Comment thoughtfully on their posts and share their content when relevant, which helps you build goodwill and visibility.

Join Instagram groups or participate in hashtag communities related to real estate and your local area to connect with like-minded professionals.

Use Direct Messages (DMs) to introduce yourself, offer value, or propose collaborations like co-hosted events or cross-promotions.

Attend and promote local events on Instagram to network offline and then share highlights online to strengthen those connections.

Consistent, genuine networking helps you expand your reach, gain trusted partners, and generate more client referrals.

Page 55: Leveraging User-Generated Content for Social Proof

User-generated content (UGC) is a powerful way to build trust and credibility by showcasing real experiences from your clients and followers.

Encourage satisfied clients to share photos or videos of their new homes and tag your Instagram handle or use your branded hashtag.

Repost this content with their permission to highlight genuine testimonials and happy buyers, making your marketing more authentic.

Host contests or giveaways encouraging followers to share stories about their home buying or selling journey.

UGC serves as social proof, reassuring potential clients that you deliver on your promises.

It also fosters community and engagement, helping your real estate brand grow organically.

Always thank contributors and maintain ethical use of their content to build lasting relationships.

Page 56: Instagram SEO Techniques for Real Estate

Optimizing your Instagram profile and content for search is essential to increase your visibility and attract more real estate clients organically.

Start by incorporating relevant keywords in your **Instagram name** and **username**—use terms like "Real Estate," "Homes," or your city name to appear in search results.

Craft keyword-rich captions that naturally include terms your audience might search for, such as "luxury homes in [City]" or "first-time buyer tips."

Utilize **hashtags strategically**—mix popular, niche, and location-based hashtags to help your posts show up in targeted searches.

Make sure your **bio** clearly states your expertise and location with searchable keywords.

Geotag your posts and Stories to appear in location-specific searches, attracting local buyers and sellers.

Engage consistently—Instagram's algorithm Favors active accounts with high engagement.

Regularly analyse your insights to identify which keywords and hashtags drive traffic, then refine your SEO strategy.

Page 57: Creating Viral Real Estate Content on Instagram

Creating viral content on Instagram can rapidly boost your real estate business visibility, attract followers, and generate leads.

Focus on **emotional storytelling** — share compelling client success stories, surprising before-and-after transformations, or unique local neighbourhood features that resonate with your audience.

Use **trending formats** like Reels, carousel posts, or IGTV videos, and tap into popular music, challenges, or hashtags to increase reach.

Create **educational content** that solves common problems, like "5 Tips for First-Time Homebuyers" or "How to Spot a Great Investment Property."

Incorporate **eye-catching visuals** with vibrant images or videos to grab attention instantly while users scroll.

Encourage engagement by asking questions, running polls, or prompting followers to share their own stories.

Collaborate with influencers or local personalities to amplify your message.

While virality can be unpredictable, consistently delivering value.

Page 58: Instagram Content Calendar for Real Estate Success

Consistency is key on Instagram, and an organized content calendar helps you plan and post regularly to grow your real estate business effectively.

Start by deciding your posting frequency—daily, every other day, or weekly—and stick to it.

Plan a variety of content types such as:

- Property listings
- Client testimonials
- Market updates
- Tips and educational posts
- Behind-the-scenes looks
- Community highlights
- Interactive Stories like polls or Q&A

Use themes or series to create anticipation, such as "Tip Tuesday" or "Feature Friday."

Schedule posts in advance using tools like Later, Buffer, or Facebook Creator Studio for efficiency.

Track post-performance to identify what content resonates most and adjust your calendar accordingly.

A well-structured content calendar keeps your Instagram active, engaging, and aligned with your business goals, helping you attract and retain followers who become clients.

Page 59: Using Instagram Insights to Improve Content Strategy

Instagram Insights is a powerful tool that helps you understand your audience and optimize your real estate content for better engagement and growth.

Access Insights from your business profile to see detailed metrics like:

- **Follower demographics** (age, gender, location)

- **Best times to post** based on when your audience is most active

- **Top-performing posts and Stories** by reach, impressions, likes, comments, and saves

Use this data to tailor your content to your audience's preferences. For example, if video posts get more engagement, focus on creating more videos showcasing listings or tips.

Pay attention to Story retention rates to identify which types of Stories keep viewers interested.

Track follower growth trends to measure the impact of your marketing campaigns.

Regularly review your Insights to refine your posting schedule, hashtags, and content themes.

By leveraging Instagram Insights, you make informed decisions that increase engagement, build trust, and ultimately grow your real estate business on the platform.

Page 60: Instagram Stories Highlights for Real Estate Branding

Instagram Stories Highlights let you showcase key aspects of your real estate business permanently on your profile, making it easier for visitors to learn about you quickly.

Organize Highlights into categories like:

- **Current Listings:** Showcase your active properties with photos, videos, and key details.

- **Sold Properties:** Build credibility by sharing success stories and closed deals.

- **Client Testimonials:** Share clips or screenshots of positive feedback.

- **Neighbourhood Guides:** Highlight local amenities, schools, parks, and lifestyle features.

- **Tips & FAQs:** Provide quick advice on buying, selling, and financing homes.

- **Behind the Scenes:** Show your daily work, team, and office culture to humanize your brand.

Design custom Highlight covers using consistent branding colours and icons to maintain a professional look.

Keep your Highlights updated regularly to reflect current listings and relevant content.

Well-curated Highlights serve as an engaging portfolio that builds trust and encourages potential clients to connect with you.

Page 61: Using Hashtags Effectively for Real Estate Reach

Hashtags are essential tools for expanding your real estate content's reach on Instagram, helping potential clients discover your posts and profile.

Use a mix of hashtag types:

- **Popular hashtags** like #RealEstate, #HomeForSale, or #HouseHunting attract broad audiences.

- **Niche hashtags** such as #LuxuryHomes or #FirstTimeHomeBuyer target specific groups.

- **Local hashtags** like #[CityName]RealEstate or #[Neighborhood]Homes connect you with local buyers and sellers.

- **Branded hashtags** unique to your business, for example, #[YourBusinessName]Properties, build brand recognition and collect user-generated content.

Limit hashtags to 10–15 per post for best results and avoid spammy overuse.

Research and update your hashtag list regularly to stay relevant with trending and location-specific tags.

Include hashtags in the caption or the first comment to keep your posts visually clean.

Monitor which hashtags bring the most engagement and leads, then optimize your strategy accordingly.

Using hashtags strategically increases your discoverability, drives targeted traffic, and grows your real estate business on Instagram.

Page 62: Creating Engaging Instagram Stories for Real Estate

Instagram Stories are perfect for sharing quick, engaging content that keeps your audience connected and interested in your real estate business.

Use Stories to:

- Showcase new listings with photos and short videos.

- Share behind-the-scenes moments like open houses or client meetings.

- Post quick tips on buying, selling, or home maintenance.

- Host polls and quizzes to interact with followers and gather insights.

- Announce events, price drops, or special offers.

- Highlight client testimonials or success stories.

Keep your Stories visually appealing using stickers, GIFs, and text overlays to capture attention.

Use the "Swipe Up" feature (available with 10k+ followers) to drive traffic directly to your website or listings.

Save important Stories as Highlights to make your valuable content accessible long-term.

Posting Stories regularly helps you stay top-of-mind, increase engagement, and build stronger relationships with potential clients.

Page 63: Using Instagram Reels to Showcase Properties

Instagram Reels offer a dynamic and engaging way to showcase your real estate properties through short, captivating videos.

Create Reels that highlight key features of a home—such as spacious kitchens, beautiful gardens, or modern interiors—to grab viewers' attention quickly.

Use trending music, effects, and creative transitions to make your Reels stand out and increase the chances of going viral.

Include quick tips about the property or neighbourhood to add value beyond visuals.

Keep Reels concise (15–30 seconds) to maintain viewer interest and optimize for Instagram's algorithm.

Add clear calls to action, like "Contact us for a tour" or "Link in bio for details," to encourage inquiries.

Reels boost your content reach by appearing on the Explore page, helping you attract a broader audience and potential buyers.

Consistently posting Reels positions you as a modern, tech-savvy agent who understands how to engage today's homebuyers.

Page 64: Collaborating with Influencers and Local Businesses on Instagram

Collaborations with influencers and local businesses can significantly expand your real estate reach and credibility on Instagram.

Identify influencers whose audience matches your target market—like lifestyle bloggers, interior designers, or local community leaders.

Partner with local businesses such as home staging companies, mortgage brokers, or moving services to create joint content, giveaways, or events.

Co-host Instagram Lives or Stories to cross-promote each other's services and tap into new follower bases.

Share behind-the-scenes content of your collaborations to showcase community involvement and build trust.

Collaborations boost engagement, provide fresh content ideas, and attract highly relevant leads interested in your real estate services.

By leveraging these partnerships, you position yourself as a connected and trusted expert in the local market.

Page 65: Instagram Live Sessions for Real Estate Q&A

Instagram Live is an excellent tool for real estate agents to connect directly with their audience in real-time and answer questions personally.

Host regular Live sessions focused on topics like buying tips, market updates, financing options, or neighbourhood insights.

Promote your Live in advance through Stories and posts to maximize attendance.

During the session, encourage viewers to ask questions in the comments and answer them on the spot to build trust and engagement.

Showcase new listings or give virtual tours live to create excitement and urgency.

Save your Live videos to IGTV so followers who missed the session can watch later.

Live sessions help humanize your brand, demonstrate your expertise, and nurture potential clients through personal interaction.

Page 66: Using Instagram DM for Lead Nurturing and Follow-Up

Instagram Direct Messages (DMs) are a powerful, personal way to nurture leads and build relationships in your real estate business.

Respond promptly and professionally to inquiries received through comments, Stories, or profile visits.

Use DMs to provide personalized property information, answer questions, and schedule viewings or consultations.

Follow up with potential clients after open houses or virtual tours to keep the conversation going and show your commitment.

Send helpful content like market updates, new listings, or buying tips to maintain interest without being pushy.

Use Instagram's quick replies feature to save time on common questions while keeping messages friendly and personalized.

Respect your leads' preferences and avoid spamming; build trust through meaningful, timely communication.

Effective DM management turns interested followers into loyal clients, accelerating your real estate sales pipeline.

Page 67: Running Instagram Contests to Boost Engagement

Instagram contests are a fun and effective way to increase engagement, grow your followers, and generate leads for your real estate business.

Create contests that encourage users to like, comment, tag friends, or share your posts to enter, increasing your content's reach.

Examples include "Tag a friend who's house hunting," photo contests of home décor, or quizzes about local neighbourhoods.

Offer attractive prizes like gift cards, free home staging consultations, or branded merchandise to motivate participation.

Clearly communicate contest rules, duration, and how winners will be selected to build trust.

Promote contests across your Instagram Stories, posts, and other social media channels for maximum exposure.

After the contest, announce winners publicly and thank participants to maintain goodwill.

Contests boost your account's visibility, increase follower interaction, and help you connect with potential clients in an engaging way.

Page 68: Instagram Ads Budgeting for Real Estate Campaigns

Setting the right budget for your Instagram ads is crucial to maximize your real estate marketing ROI without overspending.

Start by defining your campaign goals—whether it's brand awareness, lead generation, or driving website traffic—as each objective may require different budgets.

Begin with a modest daily budget (e.g., $10–$20) to test ad creatives, audiences, and placements.

Monitor performance closely during the testing phase to identify which ads deliver the best results.

Once you find winning ads, gradually increase your budget to scale successful campaigns.

Allocate more budget to highly targeted audiences—such as local buyers or specific property interest groups—to improve ad efficiency.

Consider seasonal trends and market cycles; allocate higher budgets during peak buying seasons for better impact.

Regular budget reviews and adjustments based on analytics ensure your ad spend drives maximum qualified leads for your real estate business.

Page 69: Designing Eye-Catching Instagram Ad Creatives

Eye-catching ad creatives are essential to grab attention quickly and entice users to engage with your real estate ads on Instagram.

Use high-quality, professional photos or videos showcasing your properties in the best light—bright, clear, and visually appealing.

Incorporate your brand colours, logo, and consistent fonts to reinforce brand identity.

Keep text concise and easy to read; highlight key selling points like "Spacious 3-Bedroom Home" or "Close to Top Schools."

Use strong calls to action (CTAs) such as "Book a Tour," "Contact Us Today," or "Learn More" to guide viewers.

Experiment with carousel ads to show multiple property angles or features in a single post.

Use video ads for virtual tours or quick property walkthroughs to provide immersive experiences.

A/B test different creative styles to see which resonate best with your target audience.

Well-designed ad creatives increase clicks, engagement, and ultimately, lead conversions for your real estate business.

Page 70: Targeting the Right Audience on Instagram Ads

Targeting the right audience is critical for Instagram ads to effectively reach potential real estate buyers and sellers.

Use Instagram's detailed targeting options to narrow your audience by:

- **Location:** Target specific cities, neighbourhoods, or regions where you operate.

- **Demographics:** Choose age, gender, income level, and education to match your typical buyer profile.

- **Interests:** Target users interested in home buying, real estate investing, interior design, or mortgage loans.

- **Behaviours:** Reach people who have recently moved, searched for homes, or visited real estate websites.

Create custom audiences by uploading your existing client lists or retargeting people who engaged with your profile or website.

Use lookalike audiences to find new users with similar characteristics to your best clients.

Regularly analyse ad performance and adjust targeting to improve results and reduce wasted spend.

Precise audience targeting helps ensure your ad budget attracts highly qualified leads likely to convert.

Page 71: Writing Compelling Instagram Ad Copy for Real Estate

Your Instagram ad copy plays a vital role in capturing attention and driving action—especially in a competitive real estate market.

Start with a **strong hook** in the first line to stop scrolling: Examples:

- "Dream home under ₹50L in [City Name]!"

- "Looking to buy before rates rise? Read this."

Focus on **benefits, not just features**. Instead of just listing "3 BHK, 2 baths," explain how it benefits the buyer: "Spacious 3 BHK perfect for growing families—near top-rated schools."

Include **urgency or scarcity** to drive action:

- "Only 2 units left!"

- "Book before [date] and get free modular kitchen upgrade."

Use **clear, actionable CTAs**:

- "Schedule your visit today."

- "Click 'Learn More' for full details."

- "DM us for a free consultation."

Keep your tone friendly, professional, and conversational—avoid jargon or overly formal language.

Lastly, pair your copy with relevant emojis, spacing, and bullet points to keep it skimmable and visually appealing.

Great copy connects emotionally, answers questions quickly, and pushes the audience to take the next step.

Page 72: A/B Testing Your Instagram Ads for Better Performance

A/B testing—also known as split testing—is the process of comparing two versions of an Instagram ad to see which performs better. It's a key strategy for optimizing your real estate ad campaigns.

Start by testing **one variable at a time**:

- Headline or ad copy

- Image vs. video

- Call to action (CTA)

- Target audience

- Ad format (carousel, single image, or story)

For example, test two headlines:

- "Luxury Homes in South Mumbai"
  vs.

- "Your Dream Home Awaits in South Mumbai"

Keep the rest of the ad (image, CTA, audience) the same. This way, you'll know the difference in performance is due to the headline alone.

Use Instagram's built-in tools via Meta Ads Manager to track key metrics:

- Click-through rate (CTR)

- Engagement rate

- Cost per lead

- Conversions

Run each test for at least 5–7 days and ensure your audience size is large enough to give reliable results.

Use the winning version to guide future ads, and continue testing to refine your strategy.

Consistent A/B testing helps you spend your ad budget wisely, improve campaign performance, and generate higher-quality real estate leads.

Page 73: Retargeting Strategies on Instagram for Real Estate

Retargeting is one of the most powerful Instagram ad strategies for converting interested viewers into real estate clients.

When someone visits your website, interacts with your posts, or watches your videos, they're showing interest. Retargeting allows you to serve follow-up ads specifically to those warm leads.

Here are effective retargeting strategies:

- **Website Visitors:** Show ads to users who viewed a property listing, but didn't take action. Remind them of the benefits or offer a special incentive.

- **Engaged Instagram Users:** Retarget people who liked, commented on, or saved your posts or Stories. These users are familiar with your brand and more likely to convert.

- **Video Viewers:** Serve ads to people who watched 50% or more of your Reels, Live sessions, or Stories—indicating higher intent.

- **Lead Form Drop-Offs:** Target users who opened but didn't complete your lead forms with follow-up offers or reminders.

Use personalized messaging in your retargeting ads:

- "Still looking for your dream home in Pune?"

- "Come back and explore our newest listings."

Combine retargeting with limited-time offers or urgency-based CTAs to push users toward action.

Retargeting is cost-effective, highly focused, and perfect for turning warm leads into buyers or sellers.

Page 74: Measuring Instagram Campaign Performance and KPIs

Tracking performance is critical to understanding what's working—and what's not—in your Instagram real estate campaigns.

Start by defining your **key performance indicators (KPIs)** based on campaign goals. Here are the most relevant ones:

- **Impressions & Reach:** Show how many people saw your ad. Great for brand awareness.

- **Engagement Rate:** Likes, comments, shares, and saves. High engagement indicates strong content relevance.

- **Click-Through Rate (CTR):** The percentage of people who clicked your link after seeing the ad. A higher CTR often means compelling copy and creative.

- **Cost Per Click (CPC) or Cost Per Lead (CPL):** Helps evaluate how efficiently you're using your ad spend.

- **Conversion Rate:** Tracks how many users completed a desired action—like submitting a lead form or scheduling a visit.

- **Follower Growth:** Indicates whether your content is attracting the right audience over time.

Use **Meta Ads Manager** for detailed insights and break down results by audience, placement, and device to fine-tune future campaigns.

Set benchmarks over time to understand progress and adjust strategy accordingly. Don't just look at one metric—evaluate a combination for a complete picture.

Consistent performance tracking helps ensure your marketing spend delivers the best possible return, and keeps your Instagram strategy aligned with business goals.

Page 75: Leveraging User-Generated Content for Real Estate Branding

User-Generated Content (UGC) is any content—photos, videos, testimonials—created by your clients or followers that showcases their experience with your real estate brand.

UGC builds **authenticity and trust**. When potential buyers see happy homeowners sharing their journey, it boosts credibility far more than branded ads.

Here's how to leverage UGC effectively:

- **Encourage clients to share their home-buying experience** by tagging your profile and using a branded hashtag (e.g., #SoldWithSagar).

- **Reshare client photos or Stories** (with permission) showing them in their new home, holding keys, or during move-in day.

- **Host photo contests or giveaways** asking followers to share their favorite home moments for a chance to win a prize.

- **Use video testimonials** from satisfied clients in Reels or Story Highlights to create social proof.

- **Create a UGC highlight** on your Instagram profile to show real people's journeys and feedback.

Always **credit and thank users** for their content. This not only respects their contribution but encourages others to participate.

UGC makes your brand feel human, community-driven, and relatable—qualities that help turn followers into loyal clients.

Page 76: Using Instagram Highlights to Organize Real Estate Content

Instagram Highlights are an excellent tool for keeping your most valuable real estate content easily accessible on your profile.

Unlike Stories that disappear after 24 hours, Highlights stay permanently and appear just below your bio—making them ideal for showcasing key information.

Here's how to organize effective Highlights for your real estate business:

- **Property Listings:** Create separate Highlights for "Available Homes," "Luxury Villas," "Rentals," etc., with photo or video walkthroughs.

- **Client Testimonials:** Add video reviews and thank-you messages from happy clients to build trust and social proof.

- **Virtual Tours:** Upload recorded tours of homes or neighbourhoods for prospects to view anytime.

- **Buyer Tips:** Educate your audience with bite-sized guidance on loans, down payments, or how to choose a property.

- **Behind the Scenes:** Show office life, team intros, or your daily routine to make your brand feel more personal.

- **Success Stories:** Feature before-and-after journeys, fast sales, or unique deals to highlight your expertise.

Design clean, branded cover icons for each Highlight using tools like Canva to create a polished, professional appearance.

When used well, Highlights serve as a mini-website within your Instagram profile—keeping followers informed, engaged, and impressed.

Page 77: Creating a Consistent Instagram Posting Schedule

Consistency is key to building trust, engagement, and brand recognition on Instagram—especially in a competitive real estate market.

A posting schedule helps you stay active without overwhelming your audience or burning out. Here's how to create one:

1. Choose Your Frequency

Post **at least 3–5 times per week**. Mix up your content: listings, tips, testimonials, and market updates. Stay visible, but don't sacrifice quality for quantity.

2. Use a Content Calendar

Plan your posts weekly or monthly in advance using a content calendar. Schedule specific days for themes like:

- **Monday:** Property of the week
- **Wednesday:** Client testimonial
- **Friday:** Home buying tip or reel

3. Post at Peak Times

Use Instagram Insights to discover when your audience is most active. Typically, real estate pages see higher engagement in the early evenings and weekends.

4. Leverage Tools

Use tools like **Meta Business Suite, Later, or Buffer** to auto-schedule posts and save time.

5. Include Stories & Reels

Don't just focus on feed posts. Share behind-the-scenes Stories daily and post Reels at least once a week for broader reach.

Consistency signals professionalism, keeps your audience engaged, and increases your chances of converting followers into real estate leads.

Page 78: Collaborating with Local Influencers in Real Estate

Partnering with local influencers can give your real estate brand powerful exposure on Instagram—especially in your target neighborhoods or cities.

Local influencers already have **credibility and trust** with your ideal audience. When they promote your properties or services, it feels more authentic than a direct ad.

Here's how to do it effectively:

1. Identify Relevant Influencers

Look for micro-influencers (5K–50K followers) in your area—lifestyle bloggers, interior designers, finance creators, or local celebrities. Their audience is often more engaged and geographically focused.

2. Offer Mutual Value

Propose a collaboration that benefits both sides. Offer a real estate tour, exclusive content, a referral fee, or feature them in your campaigns.

3. Promote Key Listings or Projects

Invite influencers to your property open houses or site visits. Let them create Instagram content (Reels, Stories, Lives) to generate buzz and interest.

4. Track Results

Use unique promo codes, referral links, or Instagram Insights to measure engagement, traffic, and leads from influencer collaborations.

5. Stay Authentic

Choose influencers whose tone, values, and audience align with your brand. Avoid scripted promotions; let them speak naturally about your service or property.

A well-executed influencer partnership can significantly boost your brand visibility, generate trust, and attract high-intent local leads.

Page 79: Hosting Instagram Contests to Boost Engagement

Instagram contests are a fun and powerful way to increase engagement, grow your follower base, and bring more visibility to your real estate brand.

Well-designed contests not only spark excitement but also attract potential leads. Here's how to create an effective contest:

1. Set a Clear Goal

Decide what you want to achieve—more followers, higher engagement, email leads, or traffic to your listings. Your goal will shape the contest format.

2. Choose the Right Prize

Offer a reward that appeals to your target audience. Great options include:

- A home décor voucher
- Free real estate consultation
- A branded gift hamper
- A weekend getaway (for luxury property promotions)

3. Create Simple Rules

Make it easy to enter. Common formats include:

- Like + follow + tag 2 friends

- Share this post to your story

- Comment with your dream home location

4. Use Eye-Catching Visuals

Design an attractive contest post or Reel with bold text, clear instructions, and a countdown. Highlight the prize upfront.

5. Promote the Contest

Boost the post as an ad, share it in Stories, and pin it to your profile. Collaborate with influencers or partners to extend its reach.

6. Announce the Winner Publicly

Celebrate the winner in a post or Story, and thank all participants. This builds trust and encourages more users to join future contests.

Instagram contests create buzz, build brand awareness, and convert passive followers into active participants.

Page 80: Optimizing Your Instagram Bio for Real Estate Leads

Your Instagram bio is prime digital real estate—it's the first impression visitors get and can make the difference between a scroll-past and a new lead.

Here's how to craft a powerful, lead-generating real estate bio:

1. Start with a Strong Value Proposition

Tell people who you help and how. Be clear, concise, and client-focused.

☑ Example: "Helping Mumbai families find dream homes 🏠 | 10+ years of trust"

2. Use Targeted Keywords

Include location-based and niche-specific keywords so people can find you easily in search.

☑ Example: "Pune Property Expert | Luxury Rentals & Sales"

3. Add Social Proof

Mention your experience, awards, or successful transactions briefly.

☑ "500+ homes sold | RERA Certified"

4. Include a Clear Call to Action (CTA)

Direct visitors to your next step—like a free consultation, virtual tour, or listings page.

 "👇 Book a free site visit now"

5. Optimize the Link in Bio

Use a tool like Linktree, Lnk.Bio, or your own landing page to showcase multiple links:

- Latest listings

- Client testimonials

- Booking form

- WhatsApp contact

6. Use Highlights Wisely

Your bio and profile should work together. Highlight key info like "Properties," "FAQs," or "Buyer Tips" using Story Highlights.

Keep your bio updated, direct, and client-centric. Treat it like your Instagram business card—it should answer the question: "Why should I trust this realtor?"

Page 81: Running Effective Instagram Giveaways for Local Reach

Instagram giveaways are an excellent way to generate excitement, increase local brand awareness, and build a targeted audience for your real estate business.

Here's how to run a successful giveaway that connects you with potential buyers and sellers in your area:

1. Define Your Goal

Whether it's growing your followers, boosting engagement, or collecting contact info, clarify your giveaway objective first.

2. Pick a Relevant Prize

Choose something appealing yet related to your market:

- Home décor items
- Free home consultation or appraisal
- Gift cards for local stores
- Tickets to local events or experiences

3. Create Simple Entry Rules

Common giveaway actions include:

- Follow your Instagram account
- Like the giveaway post
- Tag friends (especially local ones)

- Share the post on Stories

- Comment with their favourite neighbourhood or home style

4. Promote the Giveaway

Boost your post with Instagram ads targeting your local area and desired demographics. Share frequently in Stories and consider partnering with local influencers.

5. Engage Participants

Respond to comments and questions to keep momentum and show your active presence.

6. Select & Announce Winner Publicly

Use a random picker tool for fairness and announce winners with excitement to build trust and anticipation for future giveaways. Running giveaways consistently builds our local audience, increases engagement, and helps you connect with potential clients organically.

Page 82: Crafting Engaging Instagram Stories for Real Estate

Instagram Stories are a dynamic way to connect with your audience daily and keep your real estate brand top of mind.

Here's how to craft Stories that captivate and convert:

1. Use Visual Storytelling

Showcase property walkthroughs, neighbourhood highlights, or client testimonials through photos and videos. Keep them authentic and relatable.

2. Incorporate Interactive Features

Use polls, quizzes, and question stickers to engage viewers. Example: "Which kitchen style do you prefer?" or "Ask me anything about buying your first home."

3. Highlight Urgency and Offers

Promote limited-time deals or upcoming open houses. Use countdown stickers to create excitement and anticipation.

4. Share Behind-the-Scenes Content

Show your team at work, the home staging process, or client meetings. This builds trust and humanizes your brand.

5. Add Clear Calls to Action (CTAs)

Encourage viewers to swipe up (if eligible), DM you, or visit your profile link for more info.

6. Save Important Stories to Highlights

Organize your Stories into Highlights such as "New Listings," "Tips," "Client Wins," and "Events" for ongoing access.

By consistently posting engaging Stories, you increase visibility, nurture relationships, and generate leads from your Instagram audience.

Page 83: Utilizing Instagram Reels for Real Estate Marketing

Instagram Reels have become one of the most effective tools for real estate marketers to reach a wider audience and boost engagement.

Here's how to leverage Reels for your real estate business:

1. Showcase Property Tours

Create quick, engaging walkthrough videos highlighting key features of your listings. Use trendy music and captions to keep viewers interested.

2. Share Tips and Advice

Offer valuable home-buying tips, market updates, or financing advice in bite-sized, easy-to-digest Reels.

3. Highlight Neighbourhoods

Take your audience on a mini-tour of popular local spots, schools, parks, and amenities near your properties to give context.

4. Feature Client Testimonials

Share short clips of happy clients talking about their experience with your service to build trust.

5. Use Trending Sounds and Hashtags

Stay relevant by incorporating popular music and hashtags to increase discoverability.

6. Maintain a Consistent Style

Develop a recognizable format or theme for your Reels to build your brand identity.

Reels are favoured by Instagram's algorithm, meaning your content has a better chance of reaching potential buyers and sellers beyond your current followers.

Page 84: Instagram Ads Targeting Strategies for Real Estate

Instagram Ads allow you to precisely reach your ideal real estate audience by using detailed targeting options. To maximize your ad spend, focus on the following targeting strategies:

1. **Location Targeting:**
   Target specific cities, neighborhoods, or even postal codes where you want to find buyers or renters. This ensures your ads show only to people in your market area.

2. **Demographic Targeting:**
   Focus on age, gender, income level, and other demographics aligned with your ideal client profile. For example, target young families for suburban homes or professionals for urban apartments.

3. **Interest and Behavior Targeting:**
   Reach users interested in real estate, home buying, interior design, mortgage loans, or property investment. Instagram uses browsing behavior and engagement to identify these interests.

4. **Lookalike Audiences:**
   Upload your existing customer list and create lookalike audiences to find users similar to your best clients, increasing chances of conversion.

5. **Retargeting:**
   Show ads to users who have interacted with your profile, website, or previous ads but haven't converted

yet. Retargeting nudges interested prospects closer to making a decision.

6. **Custom Audiences:**
   Create ads for warm leads, such as email subscribers or previous inquiries, to maintain engagement and promote new listings.

Utilizing these targeting options strategically will improve your ad relevance, reduce wasted spend, and generate higher-quality real estate leads.

Page 85: Crafting Instagram Captions that Convert

A compelling caption can turn a casual scroller into a serious real estate lead. Captions give context to your posts and encourage action.

Here's how to write captions that engage and convert:

1. **Start with a Hook:**
   Grab attention in the first line with a question, bold statement, or intriguing fact.
   Example: "Looking for your dream home in Bangalore? 🏡"

2. **Tell a Story or Share Value:**
   Briefly describe the property's unique features, share a client success story, or give a helpful tip.

3. **Use Clear Call to Action (CTA):**
   Encourage followers to act — visit your website, DM for details, save the post, or attend an open house.
   Example: "DM us for a private tour!" or "Save this post for your next home search."

4. **Add Emojis & Line Breaks:**
   Use emojis to make captions visually appealing and line breaks to improve readability.

5. **Include Hashtags:**
   Add relevant local and niche hashtags at the end to boost discoverability, such as #NYCHomes, #RealEstateTips, or #DreamHome.

Good captions build connection, provide value, and gently guide your audience toward becoming clients.

Page 86: Using Instagram Analytics to Improve Your Real Estate Strategy

Instagram Analytics (Insights) provide valuable data to help you understand how your real estate content performs and how to improve your strategy.

Here's how to use analytics effectively:

1. **Track Engagement Metrics:**
   Monitor likes, comments, shares, saves, and story interactions to identify which posts resonate most with your audience.

2. **Analyze Follower Growth:**
   Watch your follower count and demographics to see if your content attracts the right audience in your target locations.

3. **Review Reach and Impressions:**
   Reach shows how many unique users saw your content, while impressions count total views. Increasing these numbers means growing visibility.

4. **Monitor Website Clicks and Profile Visits:**
   Track how many users visit your website or profile through Instagram to gauge lead interest.

5. **Evaluate Post Timing:**
   Use data on when your followers are most active to schedule posts at optimal times for higher engagement.

6. **Refine Content Strategy:**
    Focus more on the content types that perform best (videos, reels, photos) and replicate successful themes.

Regularly reviewing analytics helps you make data-driven decisions, optimize your Instagram marketing, and generate better real estate leads.

Page 87: Building a Real Estate Community on Instagram

Creating a strong community on Instagram fosters trust, loyalty, and word-of-mouth referrals—crucial for growing your real estate business.

Here's how to build an engaged community:

1. **Engage Consistently:**
   Reply to comments, answer DMs promptly, and acknowledge mentions to show you care about your audience.

2. **Create Value-Driven Content:**
   Share helpful tips, market insights, success stories, and behind-the-scenes moments that resonate with your followers.

3. **Use Interactive Features:**
   Polls, quizzes, question stickers, and live sessions invite followers to participate and feel involved.

4. **Feature User-Generated Content:**
   Encourage clients to share their home stories and repost them. This builds authenticity and community pride.

5. **Host Local Meetups or Virtual Events:**
   Organize Q&A sessions, webinars, or neighbourhood tours to connect offline and deepen relationships.

6. **Promote a Shared Vision:**
   Create a brand story that aligns with your audience's

aspirations, like helping families find dream homes or investing wisely.

Building a community turns followers into brand advocates, increasing your real estate referrals and business growth.

Page 88: Leveraging Instagram Live for Real Estate Success

Instagram Live offers a unique opportunity to engage with your audience in real-time, build trust, and showcase your expertise in the real estate market.

Here's how to make the most of Instagram Live:

1. **Plan Your Live Sessions:**
   Choose topics your audience cares about—property tours, market updates, Q&A sessions, or buying/selling tips.

2. **Promote in Advance:**
   Announce your Live session days ahead on your feed and Stories to build anticipation and maximize attendance.

3. **Engage Your Viewers:**
   Respond to comments and questions live, making the session interactive and personal.

4. **Show Authenticity:**
   Be genuine and transparent. Share behind-the-scenes moments and real client stories to build trust.

5. **Use Live to Showcase Properties:**
   Give real-time virtual tours, highlighting features and answering immediate questions from viewers.

6. **Save and Repurpose:**
   Save your Live sessions and share them on IGTV or Stories to reach followers who missed the live event.

Instagram Live helps you connect deeply with potential clients, demonstrate your knowledge, and nurture leads through direct interaction.

159

Page 89: Creating Instagram Guides for Real Estate Buyers and Sellers

Instagram Guides are an excellent way to curate valuable content in one place, making it easy for your audience to find and reference key information.

Here's how to use Instagram Guides effectively in real estate:

1. **Choose Your Guide Topics:**
   Focus on themes that help your clients—home buying tips, selling advice, financing options, neighborhood highlights, or market trends.

2. **Curate Existing Posts:**
   Compile your related Instagram posts into guides for easy navigation. For example, gather all property listings or client testimonials in one guide.

3. **Add New Recommendations:**
   Include posts from other trusted accounts like mortgage brokers, interior designers, or local businesses to add value.

4. **Write Clear Descriptions:**
   Explain the purpose of each guide and how it helps your audience, making it user-friendly.

5. **Promote Your Guides:**
   Share your guides in Stories and highlight them on your profile to increase visibility.

6. **Update Regularly:**
   Keep guides current with fresh posts and relevant information to maintain usefulness.

Instagram Guides position you as a knowledgeable resource, helping buyers and sellers make informed decisions while strengthening your real estate brand.

161

Page 90: Using Instagram Shopping Features for Real Estate Accessories and Services

Instagram Shopping isn't just for retail—it can be a creative way for real estate businesses to showcase related products and services that complement home buying and selling.

Here's how to leverage Instagram Shopping features:

1. **Set Up Instagram Shopping:**
   Link your Instagram account to a Facebook catalog with products like home décor, furniture, or real estate services such as home inspection or staging.

2. **Tag Products in Posts and Stories:**
   Showcase accessories or services in your content and tag them so users can easily view and purchase or inquire.

3. **Create a Shop Tab on Your Profile:**
   Enable a "Shop" section where followers can browse your curated products or services.

4. **Highlight Complementary Items:**
   Promote items that enhance the buying experience, such as smart home devices, security systems, or moving services.

5. **Collaborate with Vendors:**
   Partner with local businesses to feature their products, adding value for your audience and expanding your reach.

6. **Use Shopping Stickers in Stories:**
    Add interactive shopping stickers to increase product
    visibility and drive quick actions.

Instagram Shopping enhances your brand by offering holistic
solutions, turning your profile into a one-stop shop for buyers
preparing for their new home.

Page 91: Creating Consistent Instagram Branding for Real Estate

Consistency in your Instagram branding builds recognition, trust, and professionalism—key ingredients for success in real estate marketing.

Here's how to create and maintain consistent branding:

1. **Define Your Brand Voice:**
   Decide how you want to communicate—friendly, professional, approachable, or authoritative—and stick to it across posts, captions, and stories.

2. **Use a Cohesive Visual Style:**
   Choose a colour palette, fonts, and filters that reflect your brand and apply them consistently to all images and videos.

3. **Design a Memorable Logo and Profile Picture:**
   Make sure your profile photo clearly represents your business and is easy to recognize at a glance.

4. **Create Branded Templates:**
   Use templates for posts like new listings, testimonials, and market updates to maintain uniformity and save time.

5. **Stick to a Posting Schedule:**
   Regular and timely posts keep your audience engaged and expectant.

6. **Maintain Consistent Hashtags and CTAs:**
   Use a core set of hashtags and calls to action that
   align with your brand and goals.

Consistent branding differentiates you from competitors,
builds audience loyalty, and makes your real estate business
appear reliable and professional.

Page 92: Instagram Influencer Collaborations for Real Estate Growth

Partnering with local influencers can significantly boost your real estate brand's visibility and credibility on Instagram.

Here's how to collaborate effectively:

1. **Identify Relevant Influencers:**
   Look for influencers in your area with followers interested in real estate, home décor, lifestyle, or local events.

2. **Build Genuine Relationships:**
   Engage with their content and reach out with personalized messages explaining the mutual benefits of collaboration.

3. **Co-Create Content:**
   Plan posts, Stories, or Reels where influencers tour your properties, share their home-buying experiences, or highlight neighbourhood features.

4. **Leverage Influencer Giveaways:**
   Run contests with influencers to expand your reach and attract new followers interested in real estate.

5. **Track Results:**
   Monitor engagement, follower growth, and lead generation from collaborations to evaluate ROI.

6. **Maintain Long-Term Partnerships:**
   Consistent collaborations build trust and make your brand a familiar name among influencer audiences.

Influencer marketing on Instagram can open doors to new clients and create authentic buzz around your real estate listings.

Page 93: Using Instagram Stories Highlights to Showcase Your Expertise

Instagram Stories Highlights are a powerful tool to organize your best content and showcase your real estate expertise permanently on your profile.

Here's how to use Highlights effectively:

1. **Create Themed Highlights:**
    Organize Stories into categories like "Listings," "Client Reviews," "Market Tips," "Neighbourhood Tours," and "FAQs" to guide visitors.

2. **Design Custom Covers:**
    Use branded icons or images for your Highlight covers to maintain a cohesive and professional look.

3. **Update Regularly:**
    Keep your Highlights fresh by adding new Stories and removing outdated content to ensure relevance.

4. **Include Educational Content:**
    Share quick tips, buying/selling processes, or financing options to position yourself as a knowledgeable agent.

5. **Showcase Success Stories:**
    Highlight client testimonials and closed deals to build trust and credibility.

6. **Promote Events and Offers:**
    Use Highlights to inform followers about upcoming open houses, webinars, or special promotions.

By leveraging Stories Highlights, you provide visitors an easy way to access your expertise and offerings anytime, increasing engagement and lead potential.

169

Page 94: Optimizing Instagram Bio for Real Estate Business

Your Instagram bio is the first impression potential clients get of your real estate brand. A well-crafted bio can boost credibility and encourage visitors to follow or contact you.

Here's how to optimize your bio effectively:

1. **Use a Clear, Professional Profile Picture:**
   Choose a logo or professional headshot that represents your brand.

2. **Craft a Concise, Impactful Description:**
   Summarize what you do, your unique selling points, and how you help clients. Use keywords like "Real Estate Expert," "Home Buyer Specialist," or your location.

3. **Include a Call to Action (CTA):**
   Encourage visitors to take action such as "DM for listings," "Schedule a consultation," or "Visit our website."

4. **Add Contact Information:**
   Utilize Instagram's contact buttons (call, email, directions) to make it easy for prospects to reach you.

5. **Link to Your Website or Landing Page:**
   Use the website field wisely—link to your latest listings, lead capture forms, or virtual tours.

6. **Use Emojis and Line Breaks for Readability:**
   Make your bio visually appealing and easy to read.

A strategic Instagram bio acts as a powerful funnel to convert visitors into followers and clients.

Page 95: Best Practices for Instagram Hashtags in Real Estate Marketing

Hashtags increase your post visibility by connecting your content with users searching for related topics. Using the right hashtags is key for real estate marketing success on Instagram.

Here's how to use hashtags effectively:

1. **Use a Mix of Hashtag Types:**
   Combine broad hashtags (#RealEstate) with niche and local hashtags (#NYCHomes, #BangaloreProperty) for targeted reach.

2. **Research Popular and Relevant Hashtags:**
   Find hashtags frequently used by your competitors and audience, but avoid overly saturated ones where your posts get lost.

3. **Limit Hashtag Count:**
   Use between 10 to 30 hashtags per post to maintain engagement without appearing spammy.

4. **Create a Brand Hashtag:**
   Encourage followers to use your unique hashtag (#SmithRealtyHomes) to build community and track user-generated content.

5. **Place Hashtags Strategically:**
   Add hashtags in the caption or the first comment to keep your post clean.

6. **Update Hashtags Regularly:**
    Monitor performance and refresh your hashtag sets to
    stay relevant and maximize exposure.

Effective hashtag strategies boost your content's
discoverability, attracting potential buyers and sellers to your
real estate business.

Page 96: Instagram Content Calendar for Real Estate Marketing

A well-planned content calendar helps you stay organized, consistent, and strategic with your Instagram posts, essential for building a strong real estate presence.

Here's how to create an effective content calendar:

1. **Define Your Posting Frequency:**
   Decide how many posts, stories, reels, and live sessions you'll publish weekly based on your capacity and audience preferences.

2. **Plan Content Themes:**
   Rotate themes such as property listings, market updates, client testimonials, home tips, neighbourhood highlights, and behind-the-scenes.

3. **Schedule Key Dates:**
   Include important real estate events, holidays, and local happenings to align content with timely opportunities.

4. **Use Tools:**
   Utilize scheduling tools like Later, Buffer, or Hootsuite to plan and automate posts for consistency.

5. **Incorporate Engagement Posts:**
   Add polls, questions, and quizzes to encourage interaction and build community.

6. **Review and Adjust:**
   Regularly analyse content performance and tweak

your calendar to focus on what resonates most with your audience.

A strategic content calendar keeps your Instagram marketing focused and effective, driving steady real estate growth.

Page 97: How to Use Instagram Reels for Real Estate Promotion

Instagram Reels are short, engaging videos that can showcase your real estate properties and expertise in a fun, dynamic way to attract a wider audience.

Here's how to leverage Reels for real estate promotion:

1. **Showcase Property Tours:**
    Create quick walkthroughs highlighting key features, layouts, and unique selling points of your listings.

2. **Share Tips and Advice:**
    Offer bite-sized home buying, selling, or financing tips that add value and position you as an expert.

3. **Use Trending Music and Effects:**
    Incorporate popular sounds and effects to increase discoverability and make your videos more engaging.

4. **Highlight Client Testimonials:**
    Feature satisfied clients sharing their experiences to build trust and credibility.

5. **Tell Neighbourhood Stories:**
    Show local amenities, schools, parks, and lifestyle to give potential buyers a feel for the community.

6. **Include Clear CTAs:**
    Encourage viewers to contact you, visit your website,

or attend open houses by adding text overlays or verbal prompts.

Instagram Reels help your real estate brand reach new audiences and create memorable connections with potential clients.

Page 98: Engaging Your Audience with Instagram Polls and Quizzes

Instagram polls and quizzes are interactive tools that boost engagement by inviting your followers to participate and share their opinions.

Here's how to use them effectively for your real estate business:

1. **Ask Market-Related Questions:**
   Poll your audience about their home preferences, budget range, or desired neighbourhoods to understand their needs better.

2. **Create Fun Quizzes:**
   Test your followers' knowledge about real estate terms, buying processes, or local market facts to educate and entertain.

3. **Use Polls for Feedback:**
   Ask for opinions on your listings, content ideas, or upcoming events to involve your audience in your business.

4. **Promote Engagement:**
   Encourage followers to share their results or tag friends, increasing your reach organically.

5. **Share Results and Insights:**
   Post poll outcomes or quiz answers with explanations to provide value and keep the conversation going.

6. **Incorporate Stories Highlights:**
   Save your best interactive polls and quizzes in

Highlights to showcase audience engagement and educate new visitors.

Using polls and quizzes not only increases your Instagram engagement but also helps you gather valuable client insights to tailor your real estate offerings.

Page 99: Creating Instagram Ads That Convert for Real Estate

Instagram ads are a powerful way to reach targeted audiences and generate high-quality leads for your real estate business.

Here's how to create ads that convert:

1. **Define Your Objective:**
   Choose clear goals like lead generation, website visits, or brand awareness to tailor your ad strategy.

2. **Target the Right Audience:**
   Use Instagram's detailed targeting options to reach people by location, interests, behaviours, and demographics relevant to your properties.

3. **Craft Compelling Visuals:**
   Use high-quality images or videos of your properties, emphasizing unique features and benefits.

4. **Write Clear, Persuasive Copy:**
   Include strong headlines, concise descriptions, and a compelling call to action (CTA) like "Schedule a Tour" or "Contact Us Today."

5. **Test Different Formats:**
   Experiment with photo ads, carousel ads, video ads, and Stories ads to see what resonates best with your audience.

6. **Monitor and Optimize:**
   Track ad performance metrics and adjust your targeting, creatives, and budgets to maximize ROI.

Well-crafted Instagram ads help you stand out in a competitive market and attract serious buyers and sellers.

Page 100: Measuring Instagram Marketing Success with Analytics

To grow your real estate business on Instagram, it's essential to track your marketing efforts and understand what works.

Here's how to measure your Instagram success effectively:

1. **Use Instagram Insights:**
   Access built-in analytics to monitor key metrics like follower growth, post reach, impressions, and engagement rates.

2. **Track Post Performance:**
   Analyse which types of posts (photos, videos, reels, stories) get the most likes, comments, shares, and saves.

3. **Monitor Audience Demographics:**
   Understand your followers' age, gender, location, and active times to tailor content and posting schedules.

4. **Evaluate Story Metrics:**
   Check exit rates, replies, and forwards to gauge story effectiveness and adjust your strategy accordingly.

5. **Measure Ad Campaign Results:**
   Review click-through rates, conversions, and cost-per-lead to optimize your advertising spend.

6. **Set Clear KPIs:**
   Define goals like increasing followers by X%, generating Y leads per month, or boosting website visits to measure progress.

Consistent analysis helps refine your Instagram strategy, ensuring your real estate marketing drives meaningful business growth.

About the Book

In the digital-first era, Instagram has become more than just a photo-sharing app—it's a powerful real estate marketing tool. ***"100 Instagram Strategies to Grow Your Real Estate Business"*** is your ultimate playbook to turn followers into clients, likes into leads, and posts into profit.

Whether you're a realtor, broker, or real estate investor, this book equips you with proven tactics to elevate your Instagram game—from creating high-converting content to building trust, engaging your audience, and optimizing for growth.

Inside, you'll find:

- 100 actionable, easy-to-implement Instagram strategies

- Real-world insights tailored for the real estate market

- Tips on reels, stories, ads, captions, and conversions

- How to build a brand that sells properties before the showing

Your dream real estate brand is just one post away.

About the Author

Maheshwaree Budugu

She is a seasoned Digital Marketing Expert and Social Media Influencer known for her impactful work in real estate marketing. With years of hands-on experience and thousands of followers on Instagram, she helps realtors and agencies grow their presence online and build lasting client relationships.

Her work bridges creative storytelling with data-driven strategies. As the founder of Digital Bakkery, Maheshwaree empowers real estate professionals to thrive in the digital age.

Follow her journey on Instagram: @digitalbakkery0105